This work received support from the Cultural Services of the French Embassy in the United States through their publishing assistance program.

Published by Semiotext(e)
PO BOX 629, South Pasadena, CA 91031
www.semiotexte.com

Special thanks to Juliana Halpert.

Cover photograph: Hans Georg Berger, "Mathieu Lindon and Hervé Guibert at Napoleon's residence on Elba, the Villa dei Mulini, Portoferraio, 1982"

Design: Hedi El Kholti
ISBN: 978-1-63590-170-2

Distributed by the MIT Press, Cambridge, MA, and London, England.
Printed in the United States of America

Hervelino

Mathieu Lindon

Translated by Jeffrey Zuckerman

semiotext(e)

Hervelino: the word slipped into my throat.

Soon that was my nickname for Hervé, what with my habit of italianizing (if that was Italianizing) the names of my nearest and dearest when I wasn't Slavicizing them (Marcovitch, Valentinovitch, and sometimes I was Mateo or Matéovitch to Hervé). Most of the time we saw each other one-on-one: after his death, I had nobody to talk to about him using that diminutive. It's not like having said "my love" or "my dear" to a beloved now gone; the words remain, ready for others, or to be avoided. Hervelino no longer exists, meaning part of our bond. There was a lightness to it that had me wondering if it would stay that way once Hervé's death really sank in. And it's a small pleasure to remember that during a carnival in Rome, at the Villa Médicis where we were both pensionnaires toward the end of his life, Hervé got it into his head that we'd make a scene where we mimicked the Jane Birkin–Serge Gainsbourg duo singing *Raccrochez, c'est une horreur*! He'd play the poor frightened girl and I'd be the sex maniac: his idea was to call the duo we were performing as "Hervelinette and Dindono." I must have hemmed and hawed; it didn't happen. But there Hervelino was, more than ever.

Hervelino: that makes me think not so much of Hervé as of us both. The word might not seem like much but it was him and it was me, he took it for himself.

The first time we saw each other, the summer of 1978, when Michel Foucault arranged for us to meet during a little get-together, I overcame my shyness to approach him and say, since he was alone in a corner of the apartment, "Are you in time-out, Hervé Guibert?" And he must have talked about me, too, because he told me, after we'd known each other for only a few weeks, that a friend had buzzed his apartment and, when he'd asked who it was, she'd said, "Mathieu Lindon," it was completely implausible, but she'd been deluged that much with talk of me. Our names matter, those we have and those we claim. Can Hervelino be revived?

The word conjures up Italy and, for me, Italy conjures up Hervé, although not back when Hervé was born. It conjures up the start of our friendship, when Italy was still in the distance, we had no idea it might be the practically final stage. Over the years, I met up with Hervé on the island of Elba, at Hans-Georg's house or in the Santa

Caterina hermitage that he was so fond of, but the Villa Médicis was another life. Hervé came there for two years in the fall of 1987, just before learning he was HIV-positive. Eugène had won a spot the same year as him but I hadn't and I only joined them the following year: twelve months during which we were all pensionnaires. Eugène left Rome in the fall of 1989, and Hervé, too, was no longer a pensionnaire despite his best efforts (he'd applied with plenty of energy but not much hope for an additional year as an artist) and I had a year to go. We spent that year practically inseparable, the two-story place that was meant for me allowing us to live together and Hervé being all too happy to stay on the premises. He died fifteen months after we came back to Paris. But those two Roman years were, without my realizing it then since I was always oblivious, a sort of culmination of our friendship, and something of it has survived across the years.

I wouldn't have gone to the Villa if not for Hervé. It was his idea that the three of us, him and me and Eugène, be there. I'd never have applied on my own initiative and, even now, I'm grateful to him for it. All the more so considering that my friend Rachid stayed there as well from 2000 to 2001 and he'd never have thought to do so if I hadn't suggested it to him, and that I'd never have thought to suggest to him had Hervé not done so for me. At times, when I was visiting him in Rome, I told him about Hervé, and about my own stay at the Villa; it remained something strictly between us, even after he'd left the Villa. There was a sudden moment when I'd have enjoyed writing about Hervé; I wanted to but I couldn't. I don't know what to dwell on. I told Rachis that the last words the Director (who couldn't stand me) said before I left the Villa were: "You've put on some weight." There was no denying it. And Rachid: "Putting on some weight for your friend, that's wonderful. You've got to write about that." He saw my gaining as an adventure, the apotheosis of my relationship with Hervé. He made a convincing case, although I didn't rule out that my fondness of Italian cuisine might have also played some part in these kilos of affection.

I remember the "cans" during our last Roman year.

Hervé was fighting off the weight loss from AIDS. Eating was a solution. We took our breakfast separately, especially considering that our lodgings, when we each had our own, were at opposite ends of the Villa's grounds, but we had lunch and afternoon tea and dinner together every day. A daily afternoon tea (even if we only went into Rome proper about half the time) was a special thing in our thirties. We tried to keep the novelty of this activity, as if indulging in it was a game to be played. "The Balancelles," as we called the place, was what we dreamed of. La Casina dell'Orologio was on the Pincian Hill, one of the Seven Hills, which became an extension of the Villa's garden as I'd managed to get myself the key to a little door between the two parks, so that the walk, absent the steep climbs and sheer drops typical of Rome, was an especially agreeable one in going from one garden to the other. It was a bar with a patio full of what they called *balancelles* ("a free-standing swing with a cloth sunshade that usually seats two or more people and that is often installed in gardens," I read in *Le Petit Robert*, and that was exactly right), which gave the place a sense of whimsy. That was where we went every day in spring and summer, unless there was heavy rain. Joyfulness and youthfulness suffused it, and each day it was a good time. We saw children there but never other pensionnaires.

Restaurants were necessary because neither Hervé nor I cooked and so we spent our grants eating out, apart from when Eugène and Carine had us over. After I wrote *Learning What Love Means* and told about the apartment that Michel Foucault lent me on rue de Vaugirard where we'd lived, I realized that neither I nor anyone else could recall where and how we ate when we were staying there. Not a restaurant, not a bar had stuck in any of our heads, but it was clear that we hadn't had all our meals in the apartment. In Rome, I can remember so many places, Hervé had always taken note of how good various restaurants were, and that included how pleasant they were to while away hours in.

In his first year, before I turned up, Hervé had lunch alone every day at La Fiaschetteria where, in my own first year, I joined him every day apart from weekends when it was closed. We showed up early, we did our best—and succeeded—in getting the same table at the front, and the boss, Luigi, as well as the two waiters, Roberto and Ettore, were already well-acquainted with Hervé who had a phantasmally sexual connection with the less beautiful of the two. From the street, the place didn't look much like a restaurant. The dishes were family-style, plates like at home, and there were so many regulars that before long I was waving to the other diners. But in the evening it was dreary. We never had dinner there unless we'd ended up outside and the weather was too unpleasant for us to go looking for a place that wasn't packed.

L'Angoletto was chic, overlooking a relatively quiet square that I never did manage to find again after Hervé's death, although the restaurant might have closed, and Campo de' Fiori was inexpensive; each was a bit of a treat for us. Il Giardino, close to the Villa on Hervé's side, was the only restaurant open on Sunday evenings that we liked, to the point that we went there every week. When I came back ten years later with Rachid, one of the waiters immediately recognized me.

Settimio all'Arancio and the Arancio pizzeria were restaurants Hervé hadn't been to in the year before; we tried them and both became regulars. Al Gran Sasso, on via di Ripetta, was during my second year when it replaced La Fiaschetteria. It was modest and pleasant, on the wall was a fresco depicting such things as the Villa. We went there practically every day after buying the French papers that showed up at noon at the newsagent's on via della Croce; we often read them for lack of anything to talk about. It was there that, one especially quiet day, Hervé pulled me back to reality with a bewildering shout of "Clams!" At a table that wasn't quite nearby, some French diners were wondering what the *vongole* in *spaghetti alla vongole* was.

The best meals, however, were when Alain took us out on the town.

As soon as I'd settled in at the Villa, Hervé had been telling me about a pensionnaire he'd been courting since he had a car but he was no fool and every time we saw him, he suggested a place we could get to on foot, since he was wary of being used for his car which was indeed the case for most people talking to him. There was no swaying him; it wasn't long before we stopped spending time with him.

That wasn't the case with Alain. When Hervé came to the Villa, Alain was on his third year (he'd been a pensionnaire for two years then, as his girlfriend was one in turn, he stayed on, the same way Hervé later would with me). He was older than us but we'd been friends for years. He'd made sure that the duplex he was living in would be shared with Hervé, the neighbor he wanted, just as Hervé would make sure the following year that Eugène and Carine were his neighbors in turn. It was thanks to Alain that I was at the Villa. Nobody on the jury was interested in me but he'd ended up involved owing to a defection and had played up the hostility that both the head of the Villa's board of directors and the Director of the Villa had shown me so that the other jurors, some of whom weren't any more fond of me but wanted to feign impartiality, would deem it outsized. He loved cars and had several, all of them rare models, which he kept in the Villa's parking lot (a strip of lawn) and still did despite no longer having any official right to do so. Rome had charmed him so utterly that he'd rented an apartment there, where he spent quite a bit of time. He had no qualms about being used for his car which he in fact freely proposed; sometimes he'd loan it to us on the weekend for a drive by one lake or another near Rome where we'd have lunch or dinner after a swim. Those were glorious days, vacations the way a kid thought of them, when there was a whole other life to be lived.

Generally his girlfriend Danièle sat up front with Alain while Hervé and I were in the back, but those were vintage cars that he'd bought on the cheap and had to fix up, so there was only space for one passenger, and that was in the rear. Hervé and I were squeezed together, it was uncomfortable but it was still wonderful—that too felt like a childhood vacation. Especially since Alain was always reminding us about some other drive the four of us had taken in less delightful circumstances but which had still given us a good laugh.

From Paris he had driven us to dinner at one of those famous old open-air cafés on the banks of the Marne. It'd been such a lovely evening, and around midnight we set out to find the car that Alain, who hadn't found a parking spot nearby, had had to leave a few hundred meters off, and when he started the engine it became clear that one of the tires had burst. When we got out to see the problem, we found out that all four of them had. Apparently it'd been blocking the way out of someone's garage and the owner had gotten his comeuppance. So there we were, four idiots in the night on a corner in the middle of nowhere. Alain was utterly perfect, he didn't look the least bit angry but he had a few choice words about human nature, and he somehow found a phone booth where he called a tow truck which came to get us at an increasingly late hour and brought us to some random place where we could get back to Paris (if it had been willing to tow us there). But, just like with Alain's fancy cars, there wasn't any space to sit behind the tow-truck driver. We couldn't squeeze all five of us side-by-side up front and I ended up in Hervé's lap. What Alain really got a kick out of, despite the circumstances, and loved regaling us with later on, never mind that we'd been right there beside him, and far less amused by the matter (he'd been next to the tow truck driver so he'd had a front-row seat to everyone's reactions), was that Hervé, who was worried about my uncomfortable perch on his lap, had asked me if I was all right, and that the driver was as shocked as could be when I'd calmly replied, "My darling, this is exquisite." Alain and Danièle must have been just as convinced, right then and later in Rome as well, that Hervé and I were lovers—but that couldn't be farther from the truth.

It was in front of one of Alain's students—Alain also taught photography and film on the side—that Hervé and I had our first fight in Rome. A few weeks after my (and his) arrival, we were headed out to dinner with this student and his girlfriend; the two of them were younger than us and had a car. We were trying to find a restaurant far from the Villa but still in Rome proper that Hervé had heard only the best things about. He was the only one who knew the city, which made him a backseat driver. But we really were lost. There must have been streets with the same name, it was clear that we didn't know where we were and my patience was wearing thin and my wariness had me saying all sorts of things (I didn't like that we were getting farther away, I wanted to be able to get home myself, why should we bother with something new with all the things that could go wrong with anything unknown when we already had plenty of tried-and-true options?) and I was being sardonic but it was bordering on snarkiness, and Hervé finally blew up. To be honest, I don't remember exactly how things turned out, but the next day, with that spat behind us, the whole trip gave us a great story to laugh over, and we had a feeling our friends-for-an-evening had clocked us as the sort of couple to steer clear of lest they get hit by a stray bullet or two. In any case, we never had dinner with them again; they were collateral damage from our argument.

We had lunch and tea and dinner so often that there was no way we wouldn't get sick of eating together. There were days we called each other on the Villa phone system two dozen times; there were days we couldn't stand each other anymore.

Anyway, the cans. Eating in Rome was no help. Hervé got thinner and thinner. It got even more noticeable each year. When he lived in my apartment, his treatment included taking something that appeared to be a dairy product but wasn't (it was white and seemed to have that consistency) and it came in containers that looked like unlabeled tin cans. Hervé must have downed two a day, without any appetite, out of sheer force of will because it looked like a real struggle to me. He couldn't do it in secret the way he would have with a pill. I called those "the cans" because that was a way to talk about them without going into details, just knowing that he had to drink them was enough for me. And despite their real and symbolic weight, there was something lighthearted about "the cans," we could say "the cans, the cans" if there was a moment of forgetfulness, the same way someone might say "the contracts, the contracts" to summon up those good Gaston Lagaffe comic strips.

I needed that lightheartedness, often did even though that was no help in facing up to the worst. Rome and Hervé's death were two sides of the same coin, for him just as much for me. He came to the Villa just before learning he was HIV-positive and when I arrived a year later his illness was well underway even if, because I saw him so often (even back in Paris during those Roman years we had dinner together constantly) I didn't notice it, unlike others who weren't so close. I was furious at the Villa groundskeeper, whom I'd been fond enough of, when, a few weeks before the end of my stay, he mentioned Hervé and how far gone he was, how ruined his face was, with such heartfelt pity, recalling that bygone time when he was so beautiful which he only knew from photos. But for me he'd always been beautiful, the ruination had no effect on his beauty, this ruination went unnoticed because I spent so much time with him talking and laughing and being together, all the more so when I didn't realize just how close he was to death. His vigor was so familiar to me, so much a part of him, that I didn't give it much thought that I was still insisting, as the Duchesse de Guermantes did with Swann, that at heart it wasn't impossible that he might bury us all. I didn't like being disabused of this notion.

Words and literature brought us together from the outset. The first time I talked to Hervé, on rue de Vaugirard, I asked him for a piece for Minuit's magazine, which I was editing. He let me have several pieces; he eventually contributed more than anyone else. He appreciated that I read his manuscripts, offered suggestions, which I was happy to do, considering that I had experience there and didn't have any ego about what came of my comments: I gave him my thoughts, and it was all the same whether he took them to heart or not.

I met Bernardo in 1986 through my novel about Jim-Courage, which he'd liked; other books resulted in other meetings, and I have the impression that, without literature, my love life from then on would have been utterly different. I've gotten to stay in a bygone age where commercial success isn't what matters most and so what I've cared about is this: there was a text for which I had this reader, a text for which I had that one, and so on. It's not a terribly long list, but my life was a hundred times better for having this reader and that reader than having thousands of readers but not them (The Jim-Courage book has had three such special readers in twenty years, not counting Hervé who was the first). It's taken writing this paragraph to realize that I have to start my calculations almost a decade further back: it was in 1978 and with Hervé that literature helped to people my love life.

As for him, he was bolder about seeking out public success; he didn't count on individual readers, and before long he wasn't able to count on having time either. When *To the Friend Who Did Not Save My Life* didn't win the Prix Médicis, which went to another Gallimard book, he took it as a personal affront. But I remember the day, a few months earlier, when his publicist called Rome, knowing that he was staying with me, and told me that his editor would call Hervé at such-and-such a time to tell him that the book was number one on the bestseller list. When the phone did ring at that time, I told Hervé I was busy so he'd pick up. What a delight it was to see his delight!

When Gallimard put out an ad for the book, writing "The First Victory of Words Over AIDS," however, unlike Hervé, that line made me uncomfortable. He'd picked his battle with his usual bravery while, personally, the success I was hoping for was that the disease would die, not him. Literature offered him a posterity, but I would rather have had him still alive.

Up until the year in Rome when he lived with me, Hervé still had a reader who wanted some part of his love life. Rodrigue was very young, barely twenty. He'd flown from Paris and his love for Hervé was too much all the time, which annoyed me the way people in love annoy those who don't love them back. To be clear, I had no involvement in this setup, although it was my apartment Hervé used for hosting him, and the only place I could go was my apartment. Hervé was happy, touched by this boy's excitement and affection and desire which I thought was ridiculous, probably out of that jealousy one inevitably feels when someone else is the object of passion. And it meant not having dinner just with Hervé but with Rodrigue as well during a stretch when our dinners had become a pleasure again, and leaving my queen bed for the little one downstairs (or had I sent them there?). But that doesn't matter. I was relieved when Rodrigue returned to Paris and Hervé made fun of me and my annoyance. At some point after Hervé's death, I got an invitation to an exhibition of Rodrigue's work. I'd have been quite happy to go if I hadn't been in Brazil, and I didn't think to see it when I was back, as if an exhibition ended on its opening night (or maybe it was a short one and had already ended) but nowadays I do regret having dropped the one connection I had with this boy whose last name I only ever saw on the invitation card and which I've forgotten. But Rodrigue himself and this Romano-Hervelino adventure I do remember well.

When Bernardo came to see me in Rome, it was I who told him that Hervé, still a pensionnaire then, had AIDS. *To the Friend Who Did Not Save My Life*, which would make that news public to, among others, the whole Villa, wasn't out yet. One day, when we went out for lunch, Hervé told us that the night before he'd been at a club I'd refused to come with him to (as with the restaurant Alain's student had driven us to, I didn't want to get lost and not know how to get home easily in a country where I didn't speak the language) and had brought home a boy for the night. Bernardo didn't say a thing but gave him such a look that Hervé could tell just how indignant he was to hear that he'd potentially contaminated someone, which was a concern I'd never felt. Back then, there was a TV ad for head lice lotion that was always on and that bragged about its effectiveness with a cartoon of the horrible fate that awaited those parasites or whatnot being crushed by that utterly cruel adversary. It ended with the vanquished pest sighing, with its dying breath, in a shrill silly voice, "Murderer!" "Murderer!" and that line became a running joke between

Bernardo and me once he'd realized that Hervé had clearly taken every necessary precaution.

During his stay at the Villa, Hervé wrote and published two books that had a huge impact there—and beyond. *Incognito* told of his arrival and first year at the Académie (I say the Villa, but its actual name is the French Academy in Rome, l'Académie de France à Rome); it's his most openly comic novel and it shows just how stupid we could be, even though I only had cameos, since, during the stretch it described, I wasn't a pensionnaire but an occasional visitor. Hervé told me about the book while he was writing it, reassuring me that I'd love it. I couldn't wait. But, when he gave me the manuscript to read, I was disappointed, as anyone would be after such a build-up. This disappointment wasn't much of an issue, on his end or mine. I also felt that a few components were disagreeable, and I must have made a pretty strong case considering that, when I reread this book several years after his death, I found them all gone. The truth is, because bald-faced nastiness is a fundamental component of the book, I think it's a shame that he limits it to his closest colleagues and goes easy on everyone else. But that's always been his strategy, considering that his nastiness isn't necessarily that: it only warrants being inflicted on those who really can withstand it.

For example: he tells me about one of my childhood friends who'd fallen in love with him and visited him in Rome the year I wasn't there. He tells me how this boy didn't behave himself around Thierry, Hervé's friend ("Hervé's boyfriend," I might say to stem any misunderstandings that our own friendship implied), treating Thierry like a doormat, until Hervé put a stop to it. Hervé describes this trip Thierry took in a piece he had me read, and there's no mention of my childhood friend. I tell him that on particular pages I'm afraid of coming across both that friend and everything Hervé had told me about him. And Hervé justifies this absence with: "You saw what I skipped over with Thierry. With that guy, nothing's left." To each according to his ability, his power of resistance, the affection and love bestowed upon him. To attack was to test a relationship, its steadfastness; violence was pointless when the relationship wasn't strong enough for it. (This boy is the author of the "unexpected letter" that makes Hervé cry in *Voyage avec deux enfants*. My father had known him since he was seven; Hervé names him in the manuscript, but my father had suggested, out of consideration for my friend, that the name be removed. Hervé complied, but I've come to suspect that this boy would have been happy to appear as more than an initial and that he was deprived of this pleasure but wouldn't have borne any ill will.)

I don't think we came back to Paris together for Christmas 1988. Those purportedly festive festivities notwithstanding, ever since we'd first met it was rare for us not to be together. Our lifestyles as more or less single gay men meant that we were always alone on Christmas and we were in the habit of having dinner together on the 24th, Hervé having turned up a restaurant to his taste and open that night. On the 31st, as he was always invited places and I never was, he dragged me along, such as to Thierry and Christine's place. Which meant, in 1988, I was well and truly on my own, and had to make do. Unless I've got my dates wrong, he stayed in Rome to work on what would become *To the Friend Who Did Not Save My Life*. I came to the Villa with all of Thomas Bernhard's books in translation because I was fascinated by his work and had something of an idea in my head to write about him. I convinced Hervé to read them as well and he came to my place to take a book and then bring it back when he was done so he could borrow another, as if I were a library, and that didn't displease me. Thomas Bernhard, of course, had a role to play in *To the Friend Who Did Not Save My Life*, but I didn't know just how much Michel—Michel Foucault—did, too, not until Hervé had me read his manuscript. That's different from Hervelino: we said Michel, but, once Hervé was gone, I still had enough friends who'd spent plenty of time on rue de Vaugirard that I could use that first name often, just as others kept on saying it. Michel was in *To the Friend Who Did Not Save My Life*, even if his name there was Muzil, and Hervé who was so keen to have me read *Incognito* and so certain I'd like it, was worried about this book, specifically because of Michel, of the liberty he was taking in speaking of him. It wasn't even about the details he was revealing, it was just speaking of him; he seemed scared that I might be censorious, as I tended to be in conversation but not in real life. But with each book he was wrong. He'd never been so utterly Hervelino as when he was reviving (and then killing anew) Michel who remained, even in death, an essential component of our relationship.

No sooner had *Incognito* come out than everyone at the Villa was reading it; all any of them was interested in was the Villa, even if Hervé's illness appeared between the lines. Right then, Hervé wasn't a pensionnaire anymore, meaning there was no pressure on him, but he was still around, thanks to my lodgings. It gave me a chuckle to imagine the administration trying to take its displeasure out on me, and I started a rumor that a second volume would come out, since that just might keep them at bay. Whatever the reason, they did hold back. Especially since *To the Friend Who Did Not Save My Life* was published shortly after. When the book came out, after the editorial difficulties I described in *Learning What Love Means*, it got three full pages in *Libération*, meaning that, practically overnight, Hervé's illness was public knowledge.

When we came back to the Villa, everyone looked at Hervé differently. *Incognito* might have stirred up resentment, but all that was gone now. Hervé might not have forged terribly strong bonds with all but a few pensionnaires at the Villa when he himself was one, but with those there in my second year—an especially good batch in my opinion—he did. He was so taken by Éric's work that he bought one of his photos, by Denis's work that, later on, he asked Denis to do the portrait of the "man in the red hat" he'd by then become, he was charmed by the beauty of Pierre the painter and by the affection between myself and Xavier, not to mention Marie and Jean-Yves whose books he'd been aware of—more than I'd been—before they came to Rome. Everyone took care so he didn't have to suffer any compassion, he who insisted on keeping going as always, and it was true that nothing to do with him had changed with the book's publication, especially not, by some miracle, his general health. I remember Jean-Yves saying: "Now I understand why you're so kind"—or "attentive," or "alert," I don't remember—"to Hervé." And I thought that it was incredibly kind and attentive and alert to say that (and indeed I remember that thirty years later) because that wasn't how I myself felt.

Especially since *Incognito* and *To the Friend Who Did Not Save My Life* stung sophisticated readers. Pierre, a pensionnaire during Hervé's first year who'd especially appreciated him, felt like *Incognito* had struck a nerve, while Daniel, Michel's friend, was wounded far more deeply by *To the Friend Who Did Not Save My Life* than by any barb aimed at him. One day, Hervé weighed up the reactions of each and came down in the former's favor. I laughed, I really did think it was ridiculous for him to hurt people *and* decide how badly they'd been hurt, how exactly they ought to react to his blows—that was just too much. Back then, I'd been writing books that were so fully creations of my mind that there was no way I'd ever confront this problem. These days, though, I've had to. People who I'd known would take such a line or such a page badly had decided that it wasn't worth the trouble of changing our relationship, whereas others who I'd never have imagined could be bothered were, sometimes for reasons still unclear to me. They didn't clarify why as if that were proof of greater discretion, but my suspicion was that making the reason clear would make the utter grotesqueness and baselessness of the motive clear. In other words, I laughed at Hervé when he had far more reason to laugh at me. Although these days I think what hurt Daniel about Hervé's book wasn't what he said about Michel but what he didn't: namely, that everyone who knew that the book was called *To the Friend Who Did Not Save My Life* and about Michel Foucault and who hadn't read it figured that the unhelpful friend of the title was Michel Foucault. But if it's hard to hold an author responsible for readers' interpretations of his books, it's frankly asking far too much to hold that author responsible for his non-readers' opinions. That does say something about writers, though: sometimes not reading them isn't enough—they'll strike all the same.

The more Hervé wrote, the more I didn't. When we shared an apartment after he was no longer a pensionnaire, I had my desk upstairs and, downstairs where he slept, he had a small table that he'd turned into a work table. He didn't stop writing, for example *La Chair fraîche* where the word for riffraff, *racaille*, uttered by a curé, had outsize importance, and was so rare at the time that Hervé had grown fascinated with it and would die without ever witnessing its lexicographic fate. And I wrote nothing. There's a long-past book by Hervé in which he writes that we were both in Rome and I was writing all the time while he couldn't, because I was on drugs, he wrote, or I wasn't, I don't remember which. It was a private joke that I don't bother to explain these days, he was writing the opposite of the truth, that I was on drugs if I'd stopped, or that I'd stopped if I was still on them, but I do know that in fact I was, for once, writing inversely as much as he was. All through our last months at the Villa, he never stopped writing and I never managed to begin.

When I arrived, I had a writing project. It wasn't the one I'd felt like I could best justify bureaucratically during the application process. I'd have been happy to work on that one, but I wasn't really expecting to, it was more than I could have pulled off ("it's pretentious," I'd told the jury after presenting on it, and then, to make light of my presumptuousness, "but on the other hand, I won't pull it off." I found out later that, as soon as I was out of the room, the director had declared that "it'd take a lot of work to be even more of a dick than that"). But all those projects slipped right through my fingers. I'd sit down at my desk in vain with good intentions and an idea for a book—my ambition was just to describe a tennis match—

that I would only see through many years later and by some other means. Each morning, it was beyond me to feel any interest in the previous day's work. Each afternoon, I couldn't even bring myself to care about that very morning's work. After enough months of that, I gave up. What I had was worse than a bad conscience: I didn't feel like I'd stolen my grant money, the only thing in my heart after winning the competition was a gaping void. I was in Rome where I had nothing to do but write, and write was the last thing I had any hope of doing. My second year, for an issue of the institution's magazine, the pensionnaires editing it asked for contributions from all the previous two years' pensionnaires. Hervé gave them a self-portrait he'd drawn of himself with a wolf over his face. And as for me, under the title "The Masterpiece of the Century (Work in Progress)" were a few lines that were the only ones I wrote during my stay and the first of which were: "It would seem that the conditions here are ideal for working well. But are ideal conditions indeed ideal? Because I can't."

Hervé said I was a coward for giving them that text. I could see why he thought so but it did do me good to write about my inability to write. His argument was that, for months now, we'd had an outlet of sorts for the silliness we shared and I could have used the magazine to publish the best part of our sordid inventions, and help cut the institution's prestige down to size. I've come to regret that I didn't, because I've lost the texts in question and I only recall some of them which weren't necessarily the best, meaning those that gave us the biggest laugh. The end result was a "Poetical Work" in the silliest, most childish sense of the term, a game of sorts that livened our walks to one restaurant or another. (Similarly, if not half as wild, I have a self-portrait Hervé drew when he was thinking about applying as an artist for a third year at the Villa, dedicated "to Mathieu who's so encouraged my Rubenesque visual work," which honestly had more flair than the poetical work did.) If this Poetical Work has to be summarized, it would be that rhyming was essential, no matter how terrible, so we could say, in all truthfulness, "oh, poetry / it's prett-ry." I hope I'm not sullying Hervé's literary memory by quoting a few instances of our work, because his intellect played no part in his being a (fruitful and enthusiastic) collaborator whereas mine had the lion's share of effort—although I won't have anyone accusing me of braggadocio in saying so. Our title was *Collected Poems*, which could be illuminated by the first of those poems, which I reproduce here with the line breaks that only ever accompany such artistic ambitions:

> *Poésie*
> *Réussie*
> *Poésie*
> *Réunie*

Which in English might go:

Perfected
Poems
Collected
Poems

Another poem was tailor-made for an epigraph:

A chef-d'œuvre
For hors-d'œuvres.

As the Villa was at the top of the Pincian Hill, going
out for our meals (apart from afternoon tea when we went
to "The Balancelles") meant lots of uphills and downhills.
Often, playing a game I'd known since childhood, I pretended I'd hurt myself and could only walk with a stiff leg,
limping. I remember how much of a kick we got when,
one day, Hervé put some verse to our usual routine:
"When I slip," and I shot right back, "I limp," and we had
that brilliant rhyme that so perfectly summed up the matter.
There was also the opposite of the situation with *Incognito*,
which Hans-Georg had loved while I'd had my reservations. We'd come up with this ditty that was just genius:

Bells go *Ding-dong*
Krauts go *Achtung*

And when he recited it to Hans-Georg with all his
bravado, Hervé was deflated to see his listener quiet,

which Hervé, maybe hoping it could be blamed on psychology rather than truly abominable literary quality, pinned (and I did agree) on Hans-Georg's German identity being besmirched.

And for sheer rhyme, there's no translating these two French masterpieces:

> *À Angers*
> *Comme à Tanger*
> *Il y a à boire et à manger*

As well as:

> *Ce palais*
> *Népalais*
> *N'est pas laid*

And then, as I've mentioned the phantasmal connection Hervé had with the less beautiful of the two waiters at La Fiaschetteria whom he called *le garçon-vacher*, "the cowboy," it would be criminal not to mention all those times he waxed poetic about getting whipped—*se faire cravacher*—by that "cowboy"—le garcon-vacher.

Just before reading over this book an umpteenth time, I happened upon an envelope with a few pages I'd torn out of the little notebooks I'd had back then where I'd kept a few forgotten Collected Poems about human activity, whether day-to-day—rhyming *Caramba* with *cabas*, a shopping bag that'd been stolen—or professional—"The head of Administration / got indigestion." All this silliness had brought us together the first times we'd met up (and Hervé alluded to it the first time he got to inscribe a book to me), and we kept it up despite the circumstances through those Roman years. And Hervé slipped a little of it into *Incognito*, which was how he wrongly figured I'd adore it.

At the start of my second year a pensionnaire came along who wasn't at all the silly sort. All the pensionnaires considered the Villa a steal (the lump sums were pretty decent even if they hardly compared to what an ENA graduate our age might get while working in government), but this overprivileged architect insisted that it had been a financial sacrifice for him to come, and that this was an investment so that he could bill future clients more, but right then and there, he'd have gotten more by staying home. I remember one day when, walking through the piazzale with Xavier whom I'd immediately become friends with, we came across him. Xavier wasn't a classic pensionnaire either, he was an artist in a different genre and had only been at the Villa for the last six months of my stay. Even then, he was young, almost ten years younger than me, and handsome. And he was there mainly to enjoy his stay which was unnecessary from an artistic perspective. He'd won a spot as a screenwriter and, in the meantime, not only had he written his screenplay, but it was clear that it wouldn't be he who staged the production from Rome, and, having nothing to do and none of the woe I myself felt, he could pick up girls and hang around seedier spots without any contrition. Through some sort of circumstances, he'd ended up in charge of some pool of money. Which meant that this boy, who looked unkempt while somehow remaining as elegant as ever, sauntered up to the architect looking utterly proper and said, just as amiably as he would have any other pensionnaire, "Oh, by the way, I'm still waiting for that money." And it did give me a smile to see the other man nabbed exactly like a homeless man accosting a prissy couple at the Trocadéro with onlookers and asking them, with the force of conviction, "Well, are you going to pay me back or not?" The architect was beside himself but all he could say was of course, right away, I'll take care of it. He was livid at being made a fool of in front of me, even though I'd never evinced any animosity toward him, since people are who they are.

But this whole saga got even wilder when he confessed that this pensionnaire had read *Incognito*, or at least picked up enough about it to be scared of the author, and wasn't terribly happy that Hervé should remain on the premises thanks to me. He was genuinely unnerved by the rumor I'd spread of a second volume and had said of Hervé, "if he ever makes fun of me in his book I'll break his legs"— words that were immediately the talk of the Villa. The substance and the style of those words had stunned everyone, since they'd ascribed an Ancien-Régime side to him:

he'd never stoop so low as to lay a hand on such a commoner, but he'd send his lackeys to teach him a thing or two. When Hervé bothered to think of him, he hated him, but I didn't yet—it was so overblown that I was fascinated and bewildered by such a man.

His wife was a perfect match. They made for a caricature of bourgeois couples, or rather aspirants to such because fear seemed to be their daily bread and the grande bourgeoisie wouldn't be nearly as attractive if that was what they fed on. The Spanish Steps went on too long and Hervé and I were in the habit of coming back up to the Villa by the Rampa di San Sebastianello, a shorter path that took us right to the entrance. That day, there was a storm. It was raining hard and the stone was slippery and the wind was blowing in our face. Even for me it was tough going; for Hervé, who honestly had gotten much worse, it was a real challenge to press onward. We saw the architect's wife going at a brisk pace. She said something to Hervé I didn't hear and a glare that sparked words I'd never heard out of his mouth before: "Whore. Bitch." She didn't say anything back; she just skedaddled while we tried to make our way back, which really wasn't an easy matter for Hervé. And I kept talking about the rain and the wind, discussing the trouble I was having as if such sympathy would help.

"He's going to die": that fact was there from the outset and throughout the two years of being in Rome with

Hervé. But I was always caught off-guard when I was reminded of it. That was an advantage of my stupor: I didn't fret over it, and maybe that's why we had such a good time, why we were always happy. One evening during my second year, there was a retirement party for Effisio. He was a beloved staff member who'd briefly filled in for Saïd at the porter's lodge (which at the time was used to let in people who didn't have the code and where the pensionnaires came to pick up their mail), who was the picture of elegance, whom Hervé and I weren't the only ones to adore, and whose departure was the occasion for this party. It was nice out so this was on the lawn. Former pensionnaires had come in for the occasion and Hervé, too, was there with me. *To the Friend Who Did Not Save My Life* hadn't come out yet; he and I were the only ones present who knew about his illness. We'd sat on the ground to eat and drink more comfortably. Then I got up for this or that while Hervé stayed seated. Suddenly, he wanted to get up. "Help me," he whispered at a moment when nobody else could hear him and I grabbed the hand he held out to me so he could but I was ashamed not to have suggested it myself, to have forced him to make this request and not to have realized that he was no longer able to do this himself, as if I were lacking in something, love, friendship, affection, basic solidarity whereas he had not a single word of reproach for me, only gratitude once he was upright. Maybe that's why Jean-Yves's comment after the publication of *To the Friend Who Did Not Save My Life* was as touching as the hand I failed to hold out on my own initiative, mending something in me that shouldn't have needed repair and yet did.

AIDS wasn't a label I attached to Hervé or to his work before his death. I'd been reading and rereading his earlier writings so thoroughly that, in my eyes, his identity as a writer wasn't changed one bit by *To the Friend Who Did Not Save My Life* and the subsequent books, notwithstanding their power and brilliance, notwithstanding the particular sentiments they aroused. And he didn't make a fuss: he was the sort to complain for no good reason, but when there was a good one he was quiet. He was like a soldier: in the line of fire, it's too late to have any regrets, and he'd never curse those who weren't involved. He had medicine to take, he took it, done and dusted. Except when he wrote, he wrote and wrote and wrote, like a madman.

Coming back from Paris one day my first year, he let me know that my sculptor neighbor's wife was in such a worrisome psychiatric state that the other pensionnaires had decided to take turns making sure she didn't jump out of the window—the day before, she'd tried to throw her baby through it, and so, for the time being, the infant was in other, safer hands. Out of respect for their good intentions, I let them have my apartment so they could keep watch more comfortably and I went to sleep at Hervé's. I'd been on a heroin binge in Paris, I didn't even have a milligram in Rome because, despite my habit, I'd been careful not to cross the border with any, and I turned out to be in even worse withdrawal than I'd thought possible. I couldn't sleep at night, I was in a terrible state. Hervé had realized that evening and gave me a sedative strong enough for him, leaving me with the full blister pack (I was sleeping on the downstairs couch and him the next level up). But those pills had no effect on me. I was gulping them down like candy and I still couldn't get a stitch of sleep, tossing and turning. I wasn't the one with AIDS but that morning I was the one much worse for the wear. I was ashamed. Where AIDS was fated, heroin addiction was just a scandal, a thing to feel guilty about.

Boys played a big role in our relationship from the start. When I met Hervé, we were constantly going to bars together and, despite my shyness, I was always keen on hookups even if they weren't a common occurrence; Hervé, by contrast, didn't go for guys nearly as often— sometimes, if the objects of his affections made the first move, he actually gave them the cold shoulder. Dreamboats played a role, too. I remember a poster for Gervais—an ice-cream and yogurt company—slapped on the back of a bus, where there was a kid and a huge scoop of ice cream and a slogan: "I want some of that Gervais." "I want some of that" became an inside joke, insofar as the ad seemed to be meant for people with very particular tastes. That kid looked ready to pig out. Pedophilia did get plenty of opprobrium back then, if not nearly as much as now, and while that wasn't in the least bit our inclination, we did get a kick out of making people wonder. Hervé toyed with that in his *Voyage avec deux enfants*, and I made fun of that title since, even if the protagonists weren't quite of voting age, those youths weren't *enfants*—children— not by a long shot. In any case, childhood or adolescence stopped being a touchstone since, as his readers know well, one of those "children" was Vincent whom Hervé was crazy for, with many sad woes to come.

In his Roman apartment, which was one room with a mezzanine and a very high ceiling, Hervé had hung a big portrait that he'd bought in Rome. It was a painting of a Catholic priest he called Brother Vincent because he thought the man rather resembled him, and even I, who wasn't much for figures, had to concede as much. I never did see Vincent himself in Rome during my stay (he came before). At the Villa, when we were there together, his presence as a public fantasy, public in the sense of being outside Hervé's mind or body, consisted of this painting and Alain Souchon's song *C'est bien moi* sung by Françoise Hardy, which Hervé had me listen to. "*C'est bien moi d'aimer ce garçon qui m'aime pas*," "*c'est bien moi d'avoir ce tocard dans le cœur*": That's so me, loving this boy who doesn't love me; that's so me, keeping this loser in my heart. And Vincent was a topic of conversation because I think I was one of Hervé's friends who really got along with him (heroin connected us) and that was also an opportunity to imagine lamentable states of affairs, fantasies of failure that were more the result of

Hervé's merry inventiveness than of any masochism. There was something childish about Vincent, but it wasn't because of his age.

When Rachid was at the Villa ten years after I'd left, we happened to both be there at the same time as Pierre, the other former *enfant* of the *Voyage avec deux enfants*, and his girlfriend. They had a car, they took us for a drive around a lake the way Alain and Danièle had done for Hervé and me. Rachid had a cut on his fingertip and didn't want to swim and risk infecting it. We stopped at a pharmacy so he could buy protection of some sort for that. No sooner had he gotten back in the car than he unrolled a tiny plastic sheath that covered his whole pinky. "It's like a condom for a kid," he said with a big smile and I got a chuckle out of these *voyages* and these *enfants* being so varied and so vague.

Hervé was still a pensionnaire but he was on Elba while I was in Rome. I was next to the girlfriend of a former pensionnaire at a conference like the others that the Villa was in the habit of organizing. The guest was prestigious, he was utterly respectable—that's why both of us were there—but he was unbelievably boring. I noticed a boy who was especially my type in the audience. He was clearly bored, too, enough that he finally got up and left. I was right behind him. I introduced myself. He was Brazilian, lived in Paris, and was in Rome for a few days, staying with a friend. All he wanted to know was the latest about Hervé Guibert, if he was there, where he was living. In such situations, I generally kept my head down, didn't boast about how close we were, I wouldn't have even called that boasting, but given the prospect of sex in Rome, I told him that he wasn't around but that I knew him rather well, a response that seemed to turn him off. He asked me if I was a pensionnaire myself, then what medium I worked in, then which publishing houses my books had come out from—"Minuit, P.O.L?"—convinced by my earlier answers that I had to have been published by an outfit that he, in turn, considered shitty. He was caught off-guard when I said yes. "What do you mean, yes?" "Yes, Minuit and P.O.L." Suddenly we were actually flirting and we spent the night (and several others) together. Maybe it was snobbishness that had led him to my bed, but that wasn't any of my business, it was his problem to deal with just as it was for anyone I was able to lure in despite myself. Humility or pretension? Intelligence or idiocy? I've never delved into my friends' motives. Especially considering how clear it was that knowing me was no use when it came to my father, it was such a fundamental truth for me that I couldn't imagine anyone wanting to approach me for such reasons, that would be stupid, even if the others couldn't have known that. My father being an editor might have helped my friendship with Hervé, but that they'd fallen out hadn't complicated matters.

Because this boy was so keen to meet him, we had dinner with him in Paris and he would have an afterlife in

Hervé's work when the latter gave his nickname to the doctor in *To the Friend Who Did Not Save My Life*. As for that doctor, Hervé asked me the following year to lend him my apartment while we were on Elba, which I was happy to do, since she had been of help to me both as a doctor and as a human being, and since it was common in the Villa for the apartments to circulate, just as the potential secrets did in Hervé's books. When we came back to the apartment, it was clean and tidy, in perfect shape, and in addition to a thank-you note there were chocolates and two tiny statuettes of cows that didn't match. Their artistic value was nonexistent. In my shock, I instinctively held the base of one against the base of the other and while there was nothing violent in this gesture, the result was that they both shattered, and gave us a hearty laugh, as if some inherent aesthetic judgment had just been handed down. Hervé changed doctors and when, later on, I asked him if it was because of the cows, he averred that they'd had something to do with it.

The first time I came to Rome with Bernardo, Hervé playacted his Gallimard editor in various situations: talking to him about his latest manuscript, at the barber's, with his hands all over the place and the thickest accent ever, he didn't hold back and it was absolutely hilarious. He changed editors pretty fast after that. Although one of Hervé's friends told me this story: Hervé ran into that old editor after one or another of his later books came out, and he'd asked Hervé if he'd gotten the letter mentioning the book. Just hearing that question, the way it was posed, Hervé got the feeling that the letter, which he'd never gotten, had never existed, and he—sure enough—said "Oh, yes, I got it, thank you so much. I was so happy to read it."

His first year, when I wasn't a pensionnaire yet, Hervé took the night train, the Palatino Express, to Rome. Since I lived by the Gare de Lyon, we often got an early dinner at Le Train Bleu, the fancy restaurant inside the train station. But we never did so when we were taking the train together the following year. By the time I was a pensionnaire myself, the tour operator Nouvelles Frontières had started up a Paris–Rome flight on Corsair that was both more convenient and cheaper, and that was what we went with from then on.

I always feel worthless when I can't express myself how I'd like to, and, since I didn't know Italian, I was terrified of making contact with the locals. Hervé, on the contrary, spoke well, because he enjoyed it, and he'd gotten plenty of practice with his trips to Elba. One constant quirk of his that struck me was that he didn't bother to stress syllables; he just piled up his words in a monotone as if French was flat to him. The fear I felt when conducting business in Italian (except in restaurants where I'd had no choice but to pick up quickly what the dishes were and what to say to the waiters) made life complicated. I didn't dare to deal with the dry cleaners, so I washed my clothes (and then ironed them right away) in the machine available at the Villa which was often broken or being used by other pensionnaires, which meant that I had to spend so much time with my dirty clothes, dragging them to the laundry room under Marie and Jean-Yves's and then dragging them back, still filthy. I don't remember how Hervé dealt with it, we weren't so close that we washed our dirty clothes together in the same load at the dry cleaners'.

But, with Nouvelles Frontières, he handled matters for me without any fuss. He'd already started flying when I came to Rome and had struck up a friendship with a French-speaking girl at the ticket counter by the Piazza del Popolo, which was by the Villa, and I got on well with her. Thanks to Manuela, with whom we'd had dinner and quite a few drinks, to the point that we all had a good sense of each other's love lives, going by Nouvelles Frontières was a pleasure. The one inconvenience was that the airport wasn't the big international Leonardo da Vinci–Fiumicino Airport but one that was for charter flights, Ciampino, which didn't have the same amenities, and, unless we wanted to wait hours for the Nouvelles Frontières shuttle that stayed until the last passengers had dealt with formalities and grabbed their bags, which neither Hervé nor I ever checked, we were at the mercy of cabs. The day I came to Rome, Hervé had warned me about two things: the cabs, and the gangs of Roma kids milling around the Piazza Navona who acted like they were panhandling but were actually robbing you, and had taught me the words "*va' via*" with the appropriate gestures to send them to hell. I'd internalized the lesson but, when it came to cabs, warning me about their dishonesty was a fool's errand because that didn't save me from having to use them.

The Corsair flights were different from those of standard airlines because they tried to be less awkward with their passengers. Once, I had a pilot who was especially focused on human relations. He was unbelievably verbose and just speaking over the intercom from his cockpit to say "This is your pilot and I'm wishing you a good flight that will take this long. A meal will be served during the flight." Just as in Pedro Almodóvar's film *Matador*, where the pious mother, instead of just saying grace, asks the Lord specifically to bless the soup and fish before pausing, unsure, then adding, after her maid leans over to whisper, "and the custard," so did the aircraft commander spend the whole flight nattering away, which almost felt like a safety concern; he reported that we'd be served a dinner of "grated carrots then breaded schnitzel with mashed potatoes" which he hoped we'd like "before some lip-smackingly good chocolate cake." That gave me the biggest smile and I told Hervé all about it; he so sure I'd made it all up until he met that aircraft commander on a flight and then gave his name to a character in *To the Friend Who Did Not Save My Life*. It wasn't just us who were foolishly happy; there were plenty of others.

When, ten years later, I took Rachid to Nouvelles Frontières as a new pensionnaire just as dependent on me as I'd been on Hervé, Manuela was there. She asked me what the latest was with "your friend" and didn't seem fazed that she had to express her condolences.

Sometimes I'm uncomfortable recounting things Hervé told me. But my stories last longer. Although we were the same age, for me the Villa was part of my childhood whereas for him it was the end of his life. Manuela wasn't the only Roman friend Hervé furnished me with. Before her, and even dearer to me, were Évelyne and Michelena. They were respectively assistants to the General Secretary and the Director, and we were always dealing with them. Hervé had made sure that they would be kind to me, just as I was to them, and in no time we were getting along great. The housing assigned to me wasn't ready yet when I came (they were tidied and fixed up a bit between one pensionnaire's departure and the next's arrival) and for a few weeks I stayed in temporary housing off the "passerelle," a wooden balcony—meaning in the Palais itself, up high, with a commensurately wonderful view of the garden through a huge window. The bed was on a mezzanine and I'd figured out that from the bottom of the Piazza di Spagna to my bed there were 273 steps to climb. I wasn't interested in going up and down all 273 ten times a day. But I was delighted with this temporary housing just as I was with the permanent one, and when I said as much to Évelyne at some point when she wasn't alone, Hervé told me to be more discreet because it was so typical of pensionnaires to complain that being happy aroused suspicion. Évelyne and Michelena were friends with each other and often we had lunch with them, learning a thousand little useful things about life at the Académie. That Hervé was so kind to them in what he wrote in *Incognito*, claiming that he adored them, was one of the things that had bothered me, as if it wasn't all a ruse, a bit of grandstanding: didn't he love them enough to be cruel to them on the page?

They were at my side for Hervé's death, and, the few times I've gone to Rome, whether to the Villa or not, I've met up with them. But Évelyne doesn't work there anymore. I was informed by email, as I imagine various former pensionnaires were, that there would be a reception, a huge buffet lunch, for her retirement. It was set for two weeks after my mother's death and I went. I came the night before to be sure I'd be on time in case of any flight cancellations and I stayed at a hotel nearby after going through those gardens I was so fond of at the Villa Borghese which were no longer simply connected by a gate to the Villa for me because I no longer had any keys, and security had been tightened. I listened to Mahler's first symphony on my iPhone while walking through the park; I'd never been in the habit of doing so. I had dinner alone at Il Giardino where nobody recognized me this time. Then I showed up on time at the main entrance, since I didn't have the code anymore, where a young woman at the porters' lodge let me through once I told her why I'd come. Among the staff I saw, nobody recognized me, not least of all because nobody on that staff was the same as before.

The event was well put-together. There were so many people on the loggia waiting for Évelyne to finally come out of her office. She turned up, very touched, accompanied by Michelena. I was off in a corner but, when they saw me, both were truly delighted; I was the one to be overcome with emotion. Few of the old pensionnaires had made the trip, but few of the old pensionnaires had been as close to them as Hervé and Eugène and I had. Something like a will to represent all three of us, as an ambassador of sorts, had undergirded my decision to be present, whereas, apart from one who hadn't been well-liked, every single General Secretary under which Évelyne had worked over the past quarter-century had come, even from Tokyo. They'd made a point of coming and that, too, said something deeply touching about her. The lunch was a buffet, we sat wherever we liked and Michelena and I stayed together the whole time, while Évelyne was at the high table. Michelena had always lived at the Villa. Her mother had worked there and apparently it was such a sinecure that the jobs were passed down from generation to generation, and it would have been a great disappointment if the job had gone out of the family. She was a little girl and then a teenager when Balthus was the Director and had posed for him at sittings she'd written about in a text that I was all too happy to pass along to an utterly charmed Philippe Sollers who published it in *L'Infini*. I was sure Évelyne, too, had been at the Villa since time immemorial. But she hadn't. She'd come shortly before Hervé and Eugène and I only found out at that lunch that for Michelene and her, too, we were a childhood memory, a pleasant one.

There was another Roman friend Hervé introduced me to but it didn't work out, not for me nor for her. I've already mentioned how, during my first year, at moments we couldn't stand each other and our incessant meals together anymore. But we kept going: we never got so fed up with each other that one of us had lunch or dinner without the other. When it wasn't with Eugène and Carine or Alain and Danièle, since we'd abandoned the pensionnaire with a car whose being gay we'd figured would connect us but which turned out not to be enough, it was just him and me, full stop. Apart from a Roman couple slightly older than us whose first names I've forgotten and whose relationship to Hervé I never did understand, although the wife had to have been a friend of a friend. Her husband was a mathematician. I don't know how the get-together was planned because it was through Hervé, I don't know whether it was he or they who called first. They were nice enough and good-hearted, it was a change of pace to see them but the friendship didn't take. For all their politeness, being with them wasn't enjoyable. What I remember and what really doesn't sit well with me, is the reason we stopped seeing them. Hervé told me about how he'd been on the phone with the wife and she'd been asking nosy questions: "Are you all right? Are you sure you're all right? Because you don't look well. You've gotten thinner, you know." *To the Friend Who Did Not Save My Life* had not yet come out, such probing questions into his health felt like too much for him. He informed me that we wouldn't be seeing them anymore.

The first time I came back to the Villa alone, after Hervé was no longer a pensionnaire, my second year, it was dreary. The newcomers couldn't have been kinder, though. As I went up to my apartment on the second floor, I happened upon two pensionnaires whom I hadn't met but who, having done their research, knew about me—one a new neighbor, the other a painter I got along well with—so I had them over to my place. On the ground floor of my building was Éric the photographer and his companion Patou; my despair must have been utterly clear to them because they were constantly asking me to have lunch or dinner with them, and they were so warm that just writing about it touches me again. But I was so used to those meals with Hervé and it was a huge change. And I was alone in my huge apartment, and it was October. And just as the Villa gardens are a delight in spring and summer, so, when they're in shadow, when there's no light anywhere given its cloisteredness, it could be truly morose when night fell at five and I was alone without anything planned.

After coming back with Hervé in tow, determined never to return to my place alone again, we had dinners with Éric and Patou and with Denis and Thérèse. Hervé went out yet again to the club after which *Incognito* took its name and I refused yet again to come along with him. One time, he went with Pierre, my handsome neighbor. I wavered for once about not going before holding firm before finally relenting as if it were a gift to Hervé to join him even though, as he made clear to me, he'd have been quite annoyed to be saddled with me when he went with Pierre after I couldn't be bothered to do him the favor of coming with him when he went alone. I think all the pensionnaires my second year considered Hervé one of our own. Xavier told me one morning that, to get rid of a girl he'd spent the night with after *To the Friend Who Did Not Save My Life* had come out and everyone knew about it, he'd claimed that he absolutely had to come see me because Hervé wasn't doing well that morning and that, consequently, I wasn't, either. And that easy lie really gave me a chuckle.

The progression of Hervé's illness meant that my second year in Rome felt different from my first. I've mentioned the dinners but the pensionnaires also upheld the tradition of cocktail hour. We'd be at one or another's drinking and nibbling before going out to eat, or staying in to cook for practically everyone who wasn't us. And the less we could be bothered to arrange a proper meal, the more Hervé made sure to have a nice cocktail hour. There was an *enoteca*, a wine shop that he liked just steps away from La Fiaschetteria where we stocked up. That was where he discovered Bracchetto, a sparkling wine that he and even I who was barely a fan of alcohol quite liked. That was what we always brought when we went to have drinks with someone or had people over. During my second year, Marie and Jean-Yves were the only ones I'd known from before the Villa, and Hervé got along well with them too. It's nice to recall how, after an especially good get-together, we said goodbye to Marie who was so much less reserved than usual that Hervé confided to me: "She was a bit *bracchetta*!" More than anything I remember a dinner at their place that couldn't have gone better; after Eugène left we'd hardly hoped we might be so close with any other pensionnaire. Getting back to our place was a short walk through the garden, it was a fringe benefit of those in-house invitations. It was nice out, we were feeling great. The whole year before, we'd been looking for friends to have dinner with so we wouldn't always be pestering each other. And there, after a perfect evening the likes of which we'd have paid good money for the year before, in the little yard in front of the steps leading to our apartment, Hervé said that, as lovely as this had been with Marie and Jean-Yves, it was somehow even better when we had dinner just the two of us. We'd been seeing too much of each other and suddenly not enough. The days were numbered, the future was too much for the present.

Enjoying life: I couldn't have asked for more, but I don't think I even knew to. When, in a matter of weeks in the summer of 1978, I met Gérard, Michel, and Hervé, I felt like those were friendships that would last forever and that they would help me to figure things out, to find a bit of happiness. Death made this "forever" only six years long for Michel and thirteen for Hervé, but for Gérard it's four decades and counting. Hervé had been perfectly aware of this sort of inability, of essential inconvenience that I hadn't realized but which had to have been evident to anyone close to me. For example, there was a material comfort that I didn't put any value on, which he sometimes scolded me for as miserliness and which he took advantage of on other occasions for his own comfort. I was perfectly happy, at the start of my time in Rome, for him to take me to a store so we could buy a bunch of Emporio Armani tees that I thought were pretty even though I couldn't care less about clothes, only wearing them because it wasn't done to go out completely naked, which, frankly, only my occasionally pathological modesty kept me from doing. I had no taste, in every sense of the term, when it came to clothes. I wore whatever I did have to shreds and went to buy others the way I'd buy new vacuum-cleaner bags when I'd run out.

One day, Hervé scolded me for not buying some sweater for Bernardo since it cost too much and I shot back by asking him if it was stinginess that kept him from taking heroin. To be honest I'm not sure I said anything back to him. That response did immediately come to mind, but I don't recall whether I said it out loud because it was one of those times when Hervé was in such a state that winning the argument wasn't important, and besides I've always felt like I didn't completely understand human beings, certainly not myself, and it was inevitable I wouldn't understand others and the only good in combating that would be giving psychologists of every stripe plenty to work with; I didn't waste my time trying to justify myself since I'd never be able to. (LSD only reinforced that sentiment for me: when I was on it, sometimes I could share a moment of total understanding and that was such a delight, but it was only one moment and only with that drug which just went to show how thoroughly that was the exception, not the rule.) It was hard for me to imagine the pleasure that could be brought by clothes that brought me none. It felt just as indecent to shell out so much for a sweater, as it did to argue with Hervé—especially since he knew exactly how to twist the knife. During one of my stints away from Rome, I lent my apartment to Alain who was shooting a film in the Villa. One of the actors had slept there and, when I got back to Rome, there were clean and ironed and folded sheets waiting for me beside my bed. Since my sheets only ever went into the Villa's washing machine, they'd never been ironed (I sometimes gave my tees a quick pass but I never went to such trouble for sheets). At the sight of that, Hervé immediately grabbed them and said "since you don't care about them" and I didn't protest even as I knew that those beautiful sheets were slipping through my fingers.

On our last day at the Villa, because we came back to Paris together at the end of my residency, something that shouldn't have mattered to me happened and turned out, to my shock, to really sting. I didn't want to contemplate the solemnity of the day, and Hervé was even less keen to: it was clear that he'd never set foot in this place he'd loved so dearly ever again while I, even though I'd never be a pensionnaire again, would get the chance to come back as was indeed the case in the following years. But still. As the cliché has it, it was both a chapter of our life and a chapter of our time together ending all at once, and for Hervé, it wasn't just a chapter, it was almost the end of the whole book. I'd have loved to take one last walk through the garden, the gardens of the Villa Borghese, I'd have loved to stay in the apartment just for one more minute alone with Hervé. But, even though they meant well, the other pensionnaires just kept coming in to say goodbye and Hervé kept welcoming them in, Hervé who wouldn't have had the least compunction about telling them he'd prefer a bit of space if that were the case. It was my last day at my place, at our place, and already it wasn't our place anymore. We'd called a cab for Ciampino and it was already time to meet it at the Villa's front gate. At that point Hervé was traveling with a bag that was so light I didn't even have to help him carry it.

Eugène: for him, too, the word Hervelino had meaning. It would have been quite an odd thing for me never to have used it in his presence had he not done likewise.

He and Hervé came to the Villa at the same time and, their second year, when I'd arrived, they couldn't have been more neighborly, living in a tucked-away corner of the garden in a standalone house that had been turned into a duplex.

I'd met Eugène before I ever met Hervé, through the pieces he'd sent to Minuit's magazine which I was running with Denis, himself an author discovered by Tony Duvert, with whom I'd become friends. Eugène was living in Liège at the time, we didn't see each other often but we traded many letters since we were publishing his pieces: before Hervé turned up, he was the review's steadiest contributor. Hervé, similarly, got in touch with Eugène, primarily a poet at the time, before the latter and I had connected, shortly after *Mentir*, Eugène's first novel, had come out from Éditions de Minuit. But it was later on and mainly owing to the review that their relationship grew and they finally met in person. In 1982, the second-to-last issue of the magazine, which I was editing solo, as Denis had tired of it, was a special number titled "*Une rencontre entre Eugène Savitzkaya et Hervé Guibert*" that amounted to a meeting of minds between two of the magazine's stalwarts. On the cover was a photo of Eugène taken by Hervé. The issue opened with a text by Hervé titled "Letter to a Brother in Writing," followed by an interview he did with Eugène; the portfolio was rounded out by a three-page piece I'd written about the two of them. In 2013, Gallimard published the *Letters to Eugène*, the only portion of his correspondence that Hervé had expressed openness to having published, so long as Eugène agreed.

Most of what I know about their first year together in Rome comes from *Incognito*. But, with their second year, it was wonderful for all three of us to be there, even if it was cut short for Eugène. Considering the reputation of Italian hospitals at the time, Carine wanted to have their baby back in Belgium. It would have been nice if Eugène's agreeing to leave the Villa hadn't been necessary for the two of them to give birth—her, literally, to Marin; him, literarily, to *Marin, mon cœur*. Eugène was in a relationship, Hervé and I weren't, unless we ourselves were in one of some sort in this Roman setup; our lifestyles were different, no matter how free Eugène was. Hervé said that Eugène was furious about *Incognito*, but I'd never taken his apparent anger seriously: after Hervé's death, I simply talked to Eugène about him, as if death had erased all complications that might have existed, and I never got any pushback, on the contrary.

He was the same way with my father. He and Hervé had been upset with each other for years, Hervé died on a Friday and I was in the habit of having lunch at my parents' on Saturdays. I called to cancel as soon as I heard the news but, that Saturday morning, after stopping by Thierry and Christine's, I didn't want to be alone and I went over to my parents' anyway. All I talked about was Hervé as if there'd never been any trouble, and, in fact, from my father's perspective, there wasn't. His emotion was undeniable when I told him that Hervé wanted to be buried in the Santa Caterina hermitage (which proved to be impossible, and still is), said that he found Hervé's choosing the site of his burial to be moving even as, so I later learned, he'd just found his own cemetery plot. But I could tell that my mother's hostility toward Hervé hadn't abated. They'd never met, she'd never suffered anything from him, apart from the inevitable suffering my father had endured when Hervé expressed his low or scornful opinion of him in the papers (and maybe there was something about his and my being gay). In my eyes it came down to a truth that I'd already noted and would keep on noting, that was always known to me. When one is or has been close to a major figure, and has to protect them, whether the person or that person's image, one's own personality is torn between two options: to feed the beloved's strength, or to feed the beloved's weakness.

My father had published both Eugène and Hervé, but I felt no obligation to either of them for that reason; it was something about my upbringing, about the limitless literature I'd been brought up on, that contributed to my relationship with them. Eugène was the author of *Mentir*—literally, "lying"—and the first sentence about Hervé in my *Minuit* magazine piece about the two of them went: "Hervé Guibert writes 'I' and the reader believes him." That wasn't something I personally took for granted, it was practically unheard-of. I'd been bottle-fed the Nouveau Roman and believed narrative distance was standard operating procedure. Making up stories didn't feel like lying to me, even in daily life. That could be either delightful or problematic. As a teenager, when I was late to school, I had to give an excuse when I signed in. In my head, the excuse for tardiness was "tardiness"; details were pointless. And that day, which was a nice spring day, the excuse I put down was "snowstorm on the streets." There was nothing believable about it and, in my opinion, it wasn't a lie because I didn't think for one second that anyone would believe me. But people believed it. Not as an excuse, of course, but it was as if I'd wanted to obfuscate my world, which wasn't actually my intent. I like to mess around and I suspect everyone does (because it's usually plenty of fun). But no, messing around just amounts to being a bull in a china shop, and for no good reason. Apart from it, and imaginativeness, being fun for me. So, even though plenty of guys get touchy the minute they even suspect they might be mentioned in a book, as if that would reflect poorly on them or as if showing that they were crazy about eggplant gratin amounted to a monumental indiscretion, for a long time I drew no connection between what Hervé might write about me and, well, not even actual reality but the reality he saw. It took me years to figure out that he really did think I was a penny-pincher. In a way, I never did get over it. Especially since he'd once told me, a man who'd long hated going into grocery stores, that he imagined me spending my days running from shop to shop to compare prices, and that comment really stung, but what was worse, in my opinion, was just how off the mark he was. Still, I do think that he'd scolded my father so long for his miserliness that it almost felt right to think of it as a family squabble.

One day, in my first-year Roman apartment, Hervé told me that he'd written a piece that was more or less a literary massacre, with a ridiculously over-the-top title and Thierry, Hans-Georg, and myself as the victims—and I was appalled. He hadn't been expecting that, that reaction rattled him. All I could say right there and then was that there were plenty of reviewers who didn't like me and who'd have a field day with this farce, and he just rolled his eyes or something—did it matter? I knew the argument was a weak one, I'd just said the first thing that had come to mind. He was ashamed and tried to set things right by claiming that he wanted to add some other friend into the piece but I wasn't having any of it, we weren't close enough for that, and this paradoxical consolation might have helped if I could have been con-soled. But there was nothing he could say right then; only a tiny bit of heroin would help.

Because that was the thing. I'd gotten back from Paris in horrible withdrawal. I'd had a horrible night and the day clearly wasn't going to be any better. That's always been the worst part of withdrawal for me, because, for better or for worse, I have an easier time handling the physical part than most other heroin users I know; the main effect is always psychological distress so intense that it can seem as unreal as the heaven that the drug is supposed to take you to. I want to say no grief or love has ever done such a number on me. It's as if, like a nightmarish Midas, everything my thoughts touched turned dark while my brain was in overdrive, leaving no corner of my consciousness untouched. In Paris, I fought as best as I could, reading comics, taking care not to reach out to anyone or anything that might worsen my depression which I knew would only last so long and against which there was nothing I really could do while I was in the eye of the hurricane (later on, when I decided to quit heroin, I'd learn that all I needed was a few prescribed medications to quiet this storm). And I couldn't even complain to Hervé—if I was going to the trouble of comparing, he had far more and far better things to complain about. Things were topsy-turvy, it wasn't the time for me to get into all that. Hervé, who'd been so attentive, now wasn't; Hervé, who'd been so conscientious, now wasn't. "Why are we so distant from each other?" That line in *Voyage avec deux enfants* right after he'd rattled off his absent friends really struck me. I hadn't imagined such a thing happening. It was momentary; a few seconds later it was all behind me. But still, there was no way I'd ever ask to read the piece (and he abandoned it).

The General Secretary warrants some discussion. The Villa was, above all, the Académie de France à Rome, a renowned cultural institution with all the corresponding bureaucracy and hierarchy. I myself never sensed it because the place was so tranquil, but, the year Hervé came, there was a power struggle between the Director and the General Secretary that, if *Incognito* had any truth to it, was a bitter one, and, while the particulars that Hervé had related were to be taken with a grain of salt, the pensionnaires who'd weathered it were clear that he really had hewed to the facts. By the time I showed up, however, the Director had won and the former General Secretary had turned heel and left for some place nobody was able to figure out. The first thing the new General Secretary did was meet each pensionnaire, which was well-intentioned (the Director, who wisely didn't worry himself about them, hosted a cocktail hour to welcome the new pensionnaires and then shooed them out, he didn't want to hear every single bit of gossip). Hervé had no idea whether the new one would be as disagreeable as the last whose exit he'd been tangled up in, having worked to get an op-ed piece by the pensionnaires published in *Le Monde* where the Villa wasn't cast in the best light and, given the particular hierarchy and bureaucracy of the institution, the media glare was what the higher-ups had most feared, because then the Minister of Culture might poke around in their business and that would be the end of their careers.

I had scruples, which I had no scruples about ignoring, about sharing something small that cast a pall over that year in Rome, because the new General Secretary, who was our age, wasn't actually a bad person as far as I could tell. Later on, one of Hervé's friends said it really was a shame that culturocrat had been so unprepared to deal with two rascals like us (Évelyne, who worked with him, only had good things to say about him, and Rachid too had the chance to meet him later on under better circumstances). But he didn't come into our lives with such glowing recommendations. As a second-year pensionnaire, Hervé got to meet him before I did. Right then, I was living in the Palais itself and he was supposed to come tell me all about it as soon as he was out of the man's office. I opened the door, and I'd never seen him bent over laughing like that before. He managed to get inside while giggling and it was clearly making his day to give me the rundown. The General Secretary started the conversation and told him that they'd met before, had a mutual friend. As the other man had had a position at the Opéra, Hervé asked if the friend was Patrice Chéreau, but no. Isabelle Adjani? Another well-known acquaintance? No, no. Only then— and here Hervé's face was contorted with laughter at this scene—did Hervé realize that no, their mutual friend was Thierry, Hervé's friend. And suddenly, he said, he had a clear memory of this General Secretary who at the time wasn't yet one, he was just a boy chasing after Thierry, pestering him, and Hervé had indeed met him once because, since Thierry was at his limit, Hervé had grabbed him by the collar and actually lifted him off the ground while saying "You leave him alone now!" That memory, and the fact that the General Secretary actually thought it was a good idea to bring it up again, didn't reflect awfully well on him in our opinion. That whole scene always makes me think of that entry in Jules Renard's *Journal* where a guy gets slapped in a restaurant, has to leave the place while everyone's laughing at him, and, as he's stepping outside, he asks the doorman who's bent over laughing, "you want one, too?"

The General Secretary clearly admired Hervé and maybe me but all we saw there was awkwardness. He hung around us; being gay practically forced us to be together, never mind that he eventually made a fool of himself by proposing marriage to one of the other pensionnaires' girlfriends on pretext that it would only help her career. One night, he invited us to his staff apartment, part of which the Director had sectioned off to give to the new Steward. He offered us some wine or champagne I can't remember and showed us one of those half-bottles like they have on planes and which Hervé was sure he'd snuck off a flight. He went to open it in the kitchen, out of sight, we heard the sound of glass shattering, and he came with the liquid in a small container. Hervé was delighted; he was convinced the guy had broken the bottle, mopped the floor, and wrung the mop into the container because that was just how obvious the General Secretary had made his miserliness, whether real or supposed (although there was plenty of evidence thereof) to all the pensionnaires.

What really annoyed me was that he invited himself to our lunches. But that didn't last long. He talked at us like he was at a society dinner, which wasn't how we normally talked. Since all I wanted was to be left alone, not to have to deal with the Villa hierarchy which I had no interest in nor it me, my first instinct was not to make waves so long as those lunches didn't become a regular occurrence and for him to get the message. But by the end of October I'd really had it with him. The night before, France's soccer team, instead of winning as everyone'd expected, had tied with Cyprus, killing its chance to qualify for the World Cup. I was in the doldrums that any sports fan knows well when a tragedy nobody saw coming happens, made all the worse by this World Cup taking place in Italy while I was still there, the final being in Rome, and it was all just too much for me. I was reading *L'Équipe* in that foul mood while the General Secretary was droning on in front of Hervé about the Opéra in general and I have no idea which opera in particular. Hervé was listening far more politely than I ever could have with my nose buried in the paper. And the General Secretary broke off to scold me for being a snob by reading *L'Équipe* as if he were simply boring us with his operas that I couldn't be bothered about. I was seething with fury for the rest of the meal and I told Hervé that we were *never*, never having lunch with him again.

Given how wary I generally was about all bureaucracy which I was paranoid about and kept at arm's length, it made Hervé smile that the General Secretary should get me so wound up. Just to be nice and assuage whatever fury I still had, toward the end of our stay he wrote a little thing, or at least the beginning of one, titled "The General Secretary." It was just one handwritten page that I must have lost or that Hervé must have asked me to tear up. In a comically overwrought first-person narrative, he claimed to be bewildered by just how out of place it was for him, at death's door, to be wasting his energy on writing such a piece about such a person.

As for me, there was no end to my exasperation, and I hit a new low when it came to the General Secretary. One of my friends who was a friend of his gave me a present meant for him: a book carefully wrapped in purportedly artistic photos of nude boys. His denial (purely careerist, in my opinion) that he was gay was one of the things I hated most about him (although it really wasn't my business) and I undid the wrapping to see what the book was before shoddily rewrapping it on purpose so it only gestured toward hiding what in fact it didn't hide at all anymore, and I gave the thing to the General Secretary one time when there were lots of people around. I did feel a bit bad, and told Hervé afterwards: "You'd never have done such a thing." He replied, all too kindly and rightly, "There are things I've done that you'd never have done." A sort of choir group organized by the General Secretary or someone else came together and, one night, Hervé suggested we go. I said we couldn't just show up, it was a whole performance and we'd have to stay to the end. He was quite happy to take advantage of his now-notorious illness and insist that he was tired so we could leave whenever we liked without anyone making a peep.

The funniest moments of that stretch, though, turned out not to be all that funny. Not long after *To the Friend Who Did Not Save My Life* came out, near the end of our stay, Hervé and I had just gotten back from Paris, and a pensionnaire told me that the *cameriere* had refused to come tidy up my apartment as was our right once a month, saying it was because Hervé lived there—they thought they'd catch AIDS. It was such a ridiculous thing to be scared of that I had to laugh and it was with that mindset that I told Hervé what had happened. He wasn't so amused. The second I saw the dismay on his face, I felt terrible: he'd known those *cameriere* for three years and for them to be scared really stung. They'd just, in their own way, told him, "*va' via.*" And they thought I was a vector of disease, too. I personally didn't care whether or not the place was cleaned, but it was a matter of principle. I called the General Secretary and told him that I'd been led to understand that the *cameriere* didn't want to clean my place since they were scared, can you believe it, that they might get AIDS, but that it remained the responsibility of the Académie de France to find other people so that the cleaning was done. I added—and I really did feel ashamed by this thought as I hung up on the pensionnaire who'd told me what had happened—that if otherwise I'd be writing about this in the papers (I knew working at *Libération* had been a point against me when I was applying; it was a real risk that I could bring unwelcome media attention, which I made absolutely sure never to do, and that was why I was so disheartened after Denis's remark). All the General Secretary had to say was that, actually, no, it was simply because I wasn't present that the *cameriere* didn't tidy up, that was the rules (it was, although it certainly wasn't followed). But for Hervé to be hurt like that—I wasn't having any of it. I called the Steward and five minutes later, the Director called me, the only phone call I ever got from him during my stay, to let me know that the tidying would be done right away.

Decades later, I recounted that whole saga to Agata. I'd met her in Rome through Xavier, and she'd since married him. She said that wasn't odd at all for the *cameriere*, back then the Italians didn't know the first thing about AIDS, not even her, she was eighteen at the time and she was all talk and no brains. And she told me about a moment I must not have noticed because I'd never have forgotten it if I had: after the Villa, all four of us—Hervé, Xavier, her, and me—had lunch in Paris, and Hervé noticed that she wasn't sure what the right thing to do was when it came to his AIDS, that she really was worried. So he said "ooh, that looks tasty" while staring at the salad in front of her and then stuck his fork in the strawberry garnish at the edge of her plate just to scare her out of her wits.

Hervelino: I'm really glad that word's come back to mind because everyone calls him Hervé now, even people who never knew him. That doesn't bother me with my friends and family because they've heard me call him that and it'd be odd to name him with the four syllables I'd uttered when I'd asked him if he was in time-out. But here and there, students and academics interested in his work, interviewees on the radio—none of them feel the least compunction about saying Hervé. Honestly, when it comes to those people it doesn't bother me either, they're going to do what they're going to do and they do want to show how successfully Hervé's work created a space of intimacy, that it pulled them in completely. But it's so nice to have a name of his that's all mine.

I've been trying to write about Hervé for ages. But Hervé isn't a subject, so what does it even mean to "write about"? It's a silly thing to say, but it's already starting to make sense: I don't know what it is I ought to remember. I can't.

One day, I get the idea to give my inscribed copies of Hervé's books to the IMEC, the Institut Mémoire de l'édition contemporaine where Christine (Thierry's girlfriend, the mother of their children, the woman Hervé married) had already donated his archives. So researchers interested in Hervé could make use of that, I'd explain each one with a little text because they're full of inside jokes and have some relationship to Hervé's work. After reading *The Mausoleum of Lovers*, which Christine published ten years after Hervé's death as he wished, I felt bad about not having marked up my copy, there were so many things I could have shed light on that would be lost after my death. The prospect of going through the volume again for that purpose alone wasn't one that appealed to me (but I'm sure I'll reread it someday for some other reason and I'll clarify whatever particulars I can remember). The inscriptions, however, are an easier thing in my mind. And they indeed were, even if particular allusions have slipped out of my grasp already. Besides, these short texts paint the broad brushstrokes of our friendship. And putting together those few pages doesn't make me want to go any farther. But that's not going to happen, a book about Hervé, I just can't do it.

I'm also worried that I'll repeat myself in reminiscing about Hervé after having already done so in *Learning What Love Means*. It's like with *The Mausoleum of Lovers*: I don't feel like rereading my own book just to take note of what I did or didn't already say about Hervé. It only took a minute for Corentin to convince me that it didn't matter, that I could say whatever I wanted, and besides I wouldn't be saying exactly the same things. Really, if *I* can't remember what I wrote, then it's fair to assume that other readers won't be any better. But what's there for me to say about a dearly departed? *Learning What Love Means* came out twenty-seven years after Michel Foucault's death and it'll only be even longer after Hervé's death if I do manage to finish writing this thing. I've been reading a few books where survivors recall the person they lost just after the fact. And, gosh, I really do understand them. I'd have loved to be able to write while I grieved, that'd have been some consolation, some glimmer of consolation. But not a single line came to me then. And, for some hazy reason, even as I understood that people wrote as if that could help at all, as if, in the end, I could empathize with those who mourn, I was still surprised that people could publish so swiftly. Rachid broke it down for me with just one sentence: "How could a book match someone's sorrow?" But I also get that people can publish something just so they don't have to be alone with it. "Don't you ever write about me if that happens," Rachid added, and that made me shudder because he was fifteen years younger than me and I wasn't planning on having to contemplate that. I didn't say anything because he would get mad at me whenever I talked too much about my own death, now that I'm in my sixties, as if I were overdoing it about my age. Especially since the only alternative to having gotten this old was being dead, and Michel and above all Hervé had so hoped to reach this age, I didn't think it was decent to complain about coming this far.

Of those three essential men whom I'd met in the space of several weeks in summer 1978, Gérard, Michel, and Hervé, the last one was the only one I'd ever gotten into a fight with, a real one, and not only once. With Gérard, over forty years it hasn't happened even once. With Michel, it was never a possibility for me: not only were we years apart, but I had too much admiration and respect for him. With Hervé, however, we were so close for so many reasons: we were both young and gay and single and fixated on writing. For a while I was in love with him in the most sexual sense, we were always talking, and of course that would result in frustration. In a way, that was the price to pay, frustrating one's feelings could be useful in its own way.

Setting aside that he might have upset me for good reason, I do think these days (it never occurred to me back then) that sometimes I did annoy him for no good reason. As I recall various times where he misinterpreted my behavior while, as I've already said, I didn't put much effort in trying to disabuse him of his notions, it was always in terms of a power relationship: he thought I'd be a nightmare with editors if he saddled me with the responsibility I didn't want for his posthumous publications. And I specifically didn't want that responsibility so I wouldn't have to be an editor myself in the critical sense or have to be in constant contact with an editor the way I'd been since birth because my father was one. One day, after the Villa, he said, just to make me laugh, discussing a conversation with his new editor: "I've made my Mathieu Lindon." Namely that she'd remarked that the two of them were getting on well, and he'd simply said, "as long as my books sell." That really would have been just like me, if I'd been in a position to say as much to him. I think he took it as a bit of play fighting whereas, as this part of our conversation that immediately discomfited him and only deepened the befuddlement that I then noticed, I myself felt as if I'd been forced to be honest, since I didn't want to accept a compliment that was fundamentally unwarranted. But I could hardly accuse Hervé of simply misunderstanding. He'd changed my life. It'd be a bit much to scold him for believing that I was what he'd perhaps kept me from becoming.

I see the people I love as beings so wonderful that there's nothing more kind I could do than let them meet each other. For me, the commonality between Hervé and Michel isn't that they both died of AIDS but that neither of them met Rachid and Corentin. I'll always regret that. But the biggest regret of all, upon consideration, is that Hervé and Michel never got to know me as the man I became. I won't go so far as to say that I'm a morally better person (even if the situation does in fact come down to that a bit); they never saw me happy, or at least happier than they or I might have imagined. And while they did do so a bit even after their death, it's true that Hervé taught me (as I must have done for him in my way), insofar as illness had given him wisdom beyond his years which he'd bestowed upon me, illness and the fact that he never stopped writing down his final days. He insisted at the end of *The Mausoleum of Lovers* that he had all the nostalgia of an old man but to write is a youthful thing that ages the writer swiftly.

The first sentence of this text came to me unexpectedly, while I was at the gym and wasn't thinking about it, after months and months of being unable to pull together my ideas, my memories, my sentences. To write about Hervé is to write about Hervelino and the word that I thought was just waiting to be set down on the page actually was swallowed down my throat; it's no surprise that it was so scratchy. I couldn't claim Hervé or rid myself of him; I don't even know which would be better. After *Learning What Love Means* came out (I originally wrote "Learning What I Loved Means" which isn't entirely wrong), I was invited to talk about the book and Michel Foucault here and there. I'd always take care not to step out of the role I'd put myself in, to talk about him but not his work. As I'd been at the Université de Poitiers twice, an audience member who'd come both times asked me why I was so careful not to talk about the work—there was no need, after all, to treat the audience like idiots. I responded that it was my preference, whether out of pretension or modesty, only to talk about what I alone could share. It was even more true for Hervé's work: it was with him that I could best discuss it. But, as I've already mentioned, I'm writing *after* him, and, just as I didn't want to reread myself so as to make sure I wasn't repeating myself, I didn't want to reread him to check whether I was remembering right or wrong. These aren't objective facts, everyone has their own truth, which accumulates; they're just texts. And I write in his wake.

The Villa was situated in the heart of the most touristy part of Rome and so, as pensionnaires, we were permanent tourists. That made money an issue at the time. Since we paid for everything in cash and we were always paying for things, we were withdrawing huge wads of money from the bank that we walked out of, like in the movies, with pockets stuffed full of bills because the lira had been devalued far more than the franc had and we had to take out hundreds of thousands. The pensionnaires' funds came through a branch bank on the Piazza di Spagna and we were a captive clientele. Pulling money out of one's own account was an operation involving a thousand authorizations and which, at first, I wouldn't have been able to figure out without Hervé's help because there were a thousand questions to answer and even being the bank of the Académie de France was no reason for a single member of the staff to understand a single word of French. Going there was an adventure, we could count on it taking over an hour, and in order to limit the number of repeat visits as much as possible, we withdrew increasingly large sums that correspondingly increased our fear of it all being stolen by the first pickpocket we came across in this spot where apparently they were everywhere to be found, if we were to go by the despair various tourists expressed as soon as they realized that they'd suffered what we never did. The best way not to get robbed of all this money was to spend it.

For all our snobbishness, we hardly realized just how prestigious the Villa was; we were simply happy to be there, to enjoy the locale and the money we were given, but there were plenty of stupid or hopeless pensionnaires and there was no point making allowances for the juries that had chosen us (the one that had picked Hervé had thrown me out, after all). It was a delight to spend this grant that was also a way of being honest with this gift that was utterly insensible to our feelings. Somehow, money gave an order to our days that practically no meeting ever could. Not only through meals and drinks but through all sorts of purchases: in the end, we made our way practically every day to Disco Boom, which had a name that was the full package, a store on via del Tritone (on Hervé's side of the Villa) that sold CDs. In our personal rankings, the spot edged out the Vertecchi stationery shop facing the Fiaschetteria once we were stocked up enough on paper, notebooks, pencils, markers, and other things to the point that we really had nothing else to bother with there. We bought CDs at Disco Boom by the spadeful, as if we were going for the gold, operas I've never listened to (well, I did listen to some), a complete set of Piaf CDs that turned out not to be such a great idea since Hervé couldn't believe just how uneven the whole thing was (although other full sets would be more satisfactory) . . . He may have been getting worse but the playfulness of our stay wasn't. And money played a role that both surpassed and fell short of money when, in the wake of *To the Friend Who Did Not Save My Life*'s success, he insisted on considerable publishing advances for *The Compassion Protocol* and the books that followed, all the way to the very brink of his death, which he had no hope of enjoying, even if they gave him some reassurance for Christine and Thierry, who would inherit them, but which he took some personal satisfaction in managing to secure.

Money was also connected with the welter of children at the Villa. Reportedly functionaries got a bonus based on the number of children and art historians were often functionaries whose goal was to become curators. Babies and children were an excuse not to make a swimming pool out of the water tank by Hervé's place, where they'd have drowned without even a ripple if their parents had so much as glanced away (it had a tendency to swallow up giants and was just as deep as it was wide), and where I'd have been delighted to cool off after an exhausting round of tennis (there was a court right by it). This long-winded declaration was mainly my retort to those who only talked shop as if there was some shame in fully enjoying our stay, which, for that matter, unlike Hervé, I had quite a bit of difficulty doing, even though, as this privilege had fallen to us, it felt dishonest to hide it. (When I was invited to the Villa several years later to talk about the two years I'd spent there, I read a text titled "The Tennis-Player Pensionnaire's Disappointment" which, well, I'd been very happy with, although I was the only one to be.)

There was also that day in August when Hervé's music player broke. He'd bought it in Rome, the warranty was still good, and he managed to figure out where to take it to be fixed. But it was farther than we'd expected, we'd gotten the streets mixed up, and the time too and now we were walking in the summer heat under a scorching sun. We were dripping with sweat in an unfamiliar neighborhood that didn't have a single bar, absolutely parched, we couldn't go on. It was a Phillips, since it just happened that this device that did the job was a Phillips. But the brand must have had a bad reputation at the time, or Hervé pretended to think so, and he got me laughing like crazy only to crack up laughing as well by implying that he'd wanted to save on all the wrong things and pretending that we were the heroes of some ad, two idiots lost in Rome when it was forty degrees Celsius in the nonexistent shade, or rather of some competitor's ad which was showing us wandering with this aghast voice-over: "They bought Phillips!"

The misunderstandings (if I could even call them that) I complain about were ones Hervé knew about and didn't complain about. I start writing this text one night, the next morning I wake up saying that I have to stress this confusion such that his work sometimes gets reproached for its exhibitionism when all it reveals is his courage, whereas a text that I've just read does a brilliant job of showing that. Then I realize that I haven't been reading a text about Hervé, it's a sort of waking dream, a hallucination that keeps going like when I'm on heroin. But I haven't used in decades, I haven't smoked in ages, it's just that, as soon as I've gotten started again on this text under the aegis of the word Hervelino, it suffuses me so thoroughly that even my sleep is in its service, he exists in my dreaming imagination. Literature isn't made with good intentions, it's made with courage, and Hervé's courage is so clear in his texts that its presence doesn't even stand out for some readers, they're so much more accustomed to seeing it expressed with some qualms, set off by words that help readers understand that this is indeed King Courage surrounded by his court of good intentions. And, really, it's odd to scold a writer for being exhibitionistic, even when there's good reason to.

And it's odd, too, that I'd act like I'm coming to Hervé's aid, as if he needed it, I who'd always admired his courage even in the way he advocated for his books. There's something affectionate in Hervelino, a way of taking him into these arms I'd so rarely actually taken him into. He stirred up jealousy in his lifetime which lingered beyond his death, since jealousy is capable of feeding off of anything. He was handsome, young, talented: the talent remained after his death which was enough to feed ill will. But he also had enemies as consumed by discrediting as by jealousy. In his lifetime, I didn't care about that, and he too seemed not to give it any thought apart from a good laugh. Of course they grew worse after his death and, oddly, I cared even less. Enemies isn't the right word, they're not as bad as that. A month after his death, the French broadcasting network TF1 showed *Modesty or Immodesty*, the film he made in his final months not so much about sickness as about his sick body. And something began that lives on, criticisms, sometimes coming from people I'm forced to respect, about his way of doing things, that aren't so much artistic as methodological, in a way political and which I summarize thus because that's how I understand them: "That's not how to talk about AIDS."

I think about my childhood friend erased from Hervé's books. At a soirée, Gérard had told him some silly story that had everyone laughing, but Hervé, who was obsessed with correcting everybody and everything, cut in to say: "That's not how to tell it." And I think of myself suddenly realizing that, in the distance I'd kept from him up to his death, the way he'd let me know about his being positive had intruded. It's been years since I learned about Hervé's status, which only deepened our relationship. And he'd told me with an elation that discomfited me, like a stroke of luck, that turned out splendidly, he was so happy it had happened. There's no point trotting out a wealth of psychology to discern the anguish beneath, but what's stayed with me is an instinctive response I'm hardly proud of: "That's not how to tell it."

Those who scold Hervé for how he talks about AIDS are mad at him for deeming his status fated. He didn't welcome it as a good thing but he made of it what he could. And he died of it. AIDS victims aren't only those who died of it, I've come to understand this as best as I can, I who didn't dare to see myself as one because I was alive and the greatest victims no longer were. There are indeed survivors who are victims but there's a difference between those who died and those who didn't. It's hard to speak on behalf of the dead when you're alive, and all the more so against this or that dead person. Does that surprise me? That displeases me. Why? In what way do I have a right to speak? I don't. I'm just writing that there's a being whom I loved and whom I love, him and his work.

It's also a way of paying homage to the year 1978, the summer I met Gérard, Michel, and Hervé in the space of a few weeks. Each has his own book. For Gérard, I wrote the *Jim-Courage* book in 1985. At the time my ambition, declared in the text, was to compose a paperback, for convenience, so that he could always have it with him, and I had trouble putting together this text because what I wanted to write was that I loved him, and beyond that I had nothing, and that was hardly enough for a whole book (but I managed it). When I'd finished writing it, I had dinner with Hervé who on his end had completed *My Parents* and it's the only time we had a chance to exchange manuscripts, a fair trade, which kept me from making the same old joke whenever I got one from Hervé, that I hoped I wouldn't drop it in the Seine or on the métro tracks (because he hadn't made a copy). We were each outright enthusiastic about the other's book. Hervé never got the chance to read anything of mine he liked more before he died. He kindly deemed that there should be an advertisement saying that it was the book every friend ought to inscribe to his friend.

Gérard was the hero of one of my books. And so was Michel, but what about Hervé? We got into an argument while I was writing *Jim-Courage*, because it was a few months after Michel's death and I was hooked on heroin, which helped my writing due to the warmth it brought in and which complicated my life by making me irritable when Hervé bothered me, which his phone calls always seemed to be doing when I didn't want to lose a minute of the rush when the heroin was at peak literary effectiveness. Hervé doesn't appear in *Jim-Courage*, he who would be so present in *Learning What Love Means*, because my relationship with Gérard was independent of mine with Hervé, completely different from mine with Michel. Of course I would never dare to talk about my books in the same breath as Michel's and it would perhaps be odd for me to have so few compunctions about doing so with Hervé's (but I do have some): I think he wouldn't have been able to find anything to say again there, if nothing else out of kindness.

To clarify or perhaps worsen these matters, the unexpected death (Hervé's was very much expected) of Paul Otchakovsky-Laurens on January 2, 2018, revived Hervé's death for me, an additional spur to start this text that I would so loved for Paul to have published. He told me one day with a cultivated elegance that, under special circumstances, he had turned down a manuscript by Hervé and that, as he'd rejected my first one, Michel Foucault had told him: "It's one thing to overlook a good author—but *two*!" I'm not sure that Paul Otchakovsky-Laurens wasn't embellishing the story at his own expense just to be sweet.

I'm well-acquainted with the idea that an editor can lose out on an author and that readers are only too happy to pile on once publication brings the truth to light. I could have changed my mind about *Incognito* but the text I'd formed my first opinion about isn't the one that readers saw upon publication. One day I was at an homage to Hervé with Patrice Chéreau and mentioned the reservations I'd felt when Hervé had had me read his diary (at the time there wasn't any other title) years before his death. And Patrice Chéreau had protested, being such an admirer of *The Mausoleum of Lovers* which he'd just been involved in a reading of; this annoyed me because I didn't expect an artist to have the same reaction that a mere art lover would. What I'd read hadn't been what was published and what he'd read, and I hope that my comments have, even in a small way, contributed to the shift from one text to another. More generous, in my opinion, was a friend whom I'd told about reading colleagues' manuscripts and who said that, my desire not to become an editor notwithstanding, I was, in my own way, one.

Several months after Hervé's death, when Thierry was dead as well, Christine had ended up with some of Hervé's texts and asked me what to do about particular ones. At the time, my feeling was that several should be destroyed. In his final months, Hervé had carried out numerous publications and left precise instructions for posthumous publications, and I got the impression that he'd taken such care not to leave any matters unaddressed that anything else wasn't meant to be published. "Thierry wouldn't have ever done that," Christine said.

When he gave me the manuscript of *To the Friend Who Did Not Save My Life* to read, where he talks about how Muzil/Michel asks him to destroy his infinite book in particular circumstances and about how he refuses outright, I remarked on that scene, saying that if it had been me who Michel had asked and if I'd been put in that position, I'd have done it. Because there was no question that I liked Michel even more than what he'd written, which wasn't reason enough because that goes for Hervé too. It has to amount to the same character trait I'd delighted in and which he'd described in *The Gangsters* that, at a dinner where moral dilemmas of this sort were imagined, if he learned that the one he loved most was planning a murder spree, he'd rat him out right there and then, a declaration which he wrote had cast a pall, which I wouldn't have been able to make myself (independently of the reality of my behavior should such an unlikely problem arise), but which I admired. Whenever the discussion turned to the fate of his manuscripts after his death, which I sometimes wanted the responsibility of and which I sometimes didn't, I told him, one day when he said he was definitely entrusting them to Thierry, that there was nothing to worry about, that I wouldn't get myself involved, that it didn't give me the least concern. "Well, then Thierry's screwed," he shot back as if I were hinting at a betrayal.

The last time I went to Elba, to the hermitage where Hervé wanted his body to be buried, was our final summer at the Villa. I'd come down from Rome with Bernardo who'd joined me there. At Santa Caterina there were Thierry and Christine whom Bernardo got along well with, clearing the way for her and my future relationship. And, nearby, two friends of Thierry and Hervé's, two brothers—one rich, the other not—had rented a house with their buddies. It was pretty much all guys. The rich brother came to pick me up and drive me to a tennis club where, for the only time in my life, I played on real clay courts. On the way back, we went for a quick swim. I had the galley proofs of *Extinction*, the final novel by Thomas Bernard who had passed away during our Roman stay, which I was supposed to write about for *Libération*, and I loved this book more than any other by the author, and all the same I was quite happy to use its pages, once I was done reading them, to sit down in the nice car with my soaking-wet swimming trunks without any risk of ruining the seat. I made such a big hullabaloo about it that Hervé read it, too, probably once the pages were dry (he didn't have to wait long because the book was a big one and I'd started well beforehand).

However, we often had big dinners at the hermitage, with Christine the only girl among us, and those were wonderful nights. I think that was when Hervé was starting to shoot *Modesty or Immodesty*. Just as I'd been shy and scared of walking around unfamiliar parts of Rome, so I

enjoyed doing so around Santa Caterina, in a circum-
scribed space. In the film there's a moment where a lonely
silhouette can be seen in the distance around the hermitage, and it makes me smile to think it's me. Every time
he stayed on Elba, whether it was a trip he told me about
later or when I was there myself, there'd be a few moments
when Hervé and Hans-Georg couldn't stand each other
anymore (I knew the feeling well), and the close confines
didn't help matters. I've randomly come across the letters
that I wrote to him and that I'd forgotten the very exis-
tence of (Christine gave them to me after Hervé's death)
and I can see that the exasperation on Elba is perennial
and wide-ranging since I told him in the hermitage in
1983, in response to one of his letters: "Don't choke
Thierry, that'd give you no end of trouble (and plenty
of regrets)."

Friendships circulated. After Hervé's death and
Thierry's, Antoine the tennis player and I reconnected via
Christine and he said that these transitive friendships,
born out of mutual friends, were longer-lived than
symmetrical friendships, because, with the emphasis elsewhere, there was nothing to get mad about anymore.
People didn't get mad at each other, they drifted apart, the
most typical end to friendships. I'm in touch with Hans-
Georg even if he's rarely in France. I've settled back into
calling him the name Hervé gave him but other friends of
his just call him Hans. It's always stood out to me that
Hervé and he have the same initials, given the importance

of initials in Hervé's work. Italy, intimacy: it'd be quite surprising if the word Hervelino had never popped up as well in Hans-Georg's presence, whether from me or him.

"Well, I have to," Hervé replied one day in Rome when I was feeling proud of Bernardo and him getting along so well. It was charming of him to say that, that he had no choice but to like those I liked so that we still liked each other. And he put it that way because things were indeed going well with Bernardo, otherwise he wouldn't have dared. It was a sort of transitive friendship that never fell apart and Bernardo was writing a novel, *Les Initiales*, where that final summer on Elba played a sizable role. I myself had no interest in taking a dislike to his friends and complicating life either. I had dinner alone with Thierry in Paris once, Hervé being out, but it didn't go well, it was the day Hervé's mother had found out about her own illness, Hervé had rushed to her, we never did that again. As for Hans-Georg, it was only after Hervé's death that I saw him solo, a few times. And with Bernard we never had one-on-ones. The fact is that, in this very male world, it was only with Christine that I developed a personal relationship, nourished first by this last summer on Elba, then by the relationship with Bernardo, and after that by Hervé's dying days.

In the last months of his life, in Paris, I didn't see Hervé much. In my head, he wasn't too keen on his physical deterioration being apparent to me who'd been in love with him without ever sleeping with him. As I write this, it strikes me as a weak excuse, but I wasn't giving it too much thought. We talked on the phone and I let him be the one to propose get-togethers. I remember one time I came over and in the middle of my visit he was shocked that so much time had gone by without his having seen me. I was as touched as can be (to use a cliché that had struck my neighbor the sculptor my first year at the Villa when, as we made our way between the Palais and our housing, a panorama that I kept saying so many tourists would have sold their soul for, because it was what I always felt, that it really was as beautiful as can be, my descriptive abilities hardly able to surpass these frankly expressive words). But more frequent visits didn't come of that. Over the course of our relationship, we were rarely at each other's place, we met at restaurants. I remember one evening when I came in a cab to pick him up on the ground floor of his place to go to La Coupole and it was only when he got out of the car that I realized the state he was in, far beyond his extraordinary thinness which had me thinking of Holocaust survivors; he'd slipped to the bottom of the seat, with both his hands he pulled one of his legs out of the cab, then the other, and was helped to climb out of the cab by the hand that this time I thought to hold out to him.

A few weeks later, I had Éric and Patou, from the Villa and with things to do in Paris, on my sofa bed when the phone rang at an unusually early hour. It was Hervé, in a state like I'd never heard him before. It transpired that he'd wanted to finish himself off the way he'd always set it up but it hadn't worked despite the courage he'd had in not calling for any help and despite Thierry staying with him the whole night, and the home help who'd just come was taking him to the hospital and I absolutely needed to go see him this afternoon in the hospital. No sooner had he slammed down the receiver, than I called Thierry and Christine's and got the latter, since Thierry hadn't returned yet, and I told her about the phone call and she said she'd update me as soon as she had any more information. I left my room to take a shower and ran into Éric and Patou who, hearing the phone ring and evidently seeing my face, had been sure it was Hervé who'd called, or someone with bad news for me, and they'd been ginger with their questions. I think I just said that it was Hervé, and that alone was enough.

Christine called right back, although we wouldn't possibly be seeing Hervé that afternoon. The hospital was in Clamart, which we couldn't get to without a car, and she proposed that we head there together. And so two duos drove to see Hervé: Thierry and Hans-Georg in the late afternoon, Christine and me in the morning. The first time we reached the hospital, once she'd parked and gotten out of the car, I mentioned that this desire Hervé had expressed for me to come see him was perhaps due to his state of mind right then, I didn't expect better than that and I'd have felt most comfortable if she got confirmation from him before I came in. So she did, and, when she came back, I didn't get out of the car; we just headed back to Paris.

When I told Agata about that time, in the same conversation in which she'd mentioned Hervé's fork thrust like an assault weapon into her dish, she remarked on my matter-of-factness, which I hadn't noticed: it was I who didn't want to see Hervé at the hospital. I was rattled. Because that reminded me of Thierry's fate as well. He died less than seven months after Hervé and nobody had warned him it would be so swift. And I wondered if the slowness, if that unfortunately can be said, in which Hervé had left us hadn't played some role in this swiftness: he couldn't fret about his children only retaining a single, degraded image, like the one Hervé had ultimately acquired, of his handsome self. For some odd reason, I figured it would have been in poor taste to share this sentiment with Christine until, years and years later, as I was doing my best to be as tactful as possible, I finally dared to say as much to her, to which she responded: "Of course." Maybe I was the one who didn't want to see Hervé like this, maybe it was him who didn't want me to see him like this.

From then on I went with Christine to the hospital each day and never got out of the car. We met by the Saint-Jacques métro stop and that struck me as odd too because it was at this station that Samuel Beckett lived, his building was one of the last that could be seen before the above-ground train car entered its tunnel and, back then,

I could remember which floor his apartment was on and therefore he himself was on. Samuel Beckett was so important to my father that he came to matter to me as well, back then he'd only been dead for two years (at eighty-three years old, Hervé was thirty-six and in the hospital), emotions welled up in me. Christine and I talked on the way there, on the way back, but I stayed by myself in the car in the hospital parking lot, choosing to be there without wondering about the human being there.

In Rome, I couldn't work (and it was hard, before meeting Xavier lightened matters). The easiest thing would have been to write this book, even if it would have been a different book. That didn't for one second occur to me. I never made a single note about my friends. I'd had so few friendships as a teenager that it would have been indecent of me to use one for literary purposes, friendship was for friendship's sake just as art was for art's sake and, as it happens, those were two parallel universes that wouldn't intersect until infinity: the infinity of death when it came to Hervé and Michel, and that took a good quarter-century. (The *Jim-Courage* book was a different matter: Gérard was unrecognizable, the book is a novel and came out thirty years ago, meaning it doesn't account for our relationship in those years since.) I may talk about it in the past tense, but nothing's changed. Where I see myself as a witness, I've opted for discretion. Where I see myself as an actor, it takes me time to figure out how to talk about my role. That's what actors are asked to do, isn't it? To live, rather than comment on life? I live in writing, with an intensity that I don't have when I can't work, but, in Rome, I lived with Hervé, in our particular way which isn't easy to relive.

When Christine invited me to spend December 24 at her and Thierry's place with Hans-Georg (and another guest), all of us friends of Hervé, that was bad news. That December 24 I'd spend without Hervé dying in the hospital, I was already invited over to Xavier and Agata's and I was looking forward to the evening. Too bad. I canceled with Xavier and Agata; my place was with Hervé's friends even if it would be less enjoyable. As usual, I was the first to show up. Even Thierry wasn't at home because he was at Clamart, at the hospital with Hans-Georg. Before they got back, the other guest showed up. Christine had just warned me about this other fellow. When he came to Paris, Hans-Georg slept at Thierry and Christine's, or at Bernard's, another friend of Hervé's who, being away, was also hosting a young Moroccan man he'd met in Marrakesh who'd gotten a visa to spend his Christmas vacation in Paris. Since he was alone on Christmas Eve, Hans-Georg suggested that he come and take part in ours. He didn't know any of the guests but in Morocco he'd read *To the Friend Who Did Not Save My Life*, so that had to be quite the Christmas, spending it with so many of the book's characters.

I fell head over heels for him the moment I laid eyes on him. Even so, I went home alone and it took some help from Hans-Georg, who said he'd picked up this ability to make connections from Bernard, for me to see him again three days later and for us to have sex only minutes before Christine would call me to tell me that Hervé was dead. And it was such a confluence of circumstances, as if Bernard and Hans-Georg, Thierry and Christine, all of Hervé's closest friends had gotten together to make this encounter possible, and it was as if Hervé himself had had some hand in it, an impression that I still couldn't shake even when Rachid became a pensionnaire at the Villa Médicis and I spent time with him in the apartment that had once housed Marie and Jean-Yves. Always Hervé, always Rome.

"Hervé Guibert, la mort propagande," read the headline in *Libération* announcing Hervé's death, and this reminder of his very first published book underscored his relationship to death before his illness, further discrediting in my eyes those who'd disdained how he'd welcomed his AIDS diagnosis (he did as he liked, as he could, and they did too: if opposing Hervé gave them strength, very well, so much the better, but they didn't need to disdain him). The synchrony between Hervé's departure and Rachid's arrival, even if I didn't suspect how important he'd prove to be, sent me into emotional turmoil. I was present for Hervé's body being moved in Clamart, but I didn't follow the hearse to Elba (would I have gone if it had been in

Rome?), banking on the permission Hervé had given me because we'd talked about it and I hadn't wanted to make the trip just as I hadn't wanted to make the one for the transfer of Michel's body from the Paris morgue to his family's cemetery near Poitiers.

A few days after his death, Hans-Georg told me that Hervé had planned it. He and Thierry had read the word *Mort*—death—in his diary, on the day following the morning he'd called me. Then, a few days later, he asked me if I could stop by Hervé's that Saturday; yes, that was in the cards. It wasn't *Mort* that was written, but the first four letters of my name. Stark, unadulterated death was wholly unacceptable, just a decision, a foreboding (or, on the contrary, total unexpectedness) was all anyone wanted. No sooner had death come than everything got muddled up. Soon memories weren't matching up. I feel like everyone I knew, back when I knew Hervé, knew him but not in a straightforward way, sometimes they knew about our relationship without having seen us together, despite being unaware of the whole Hervelino setup. It was enough, after Hervé's death on December 27th, for a friend to invite me to a New Year's Eve party, not because I'd be the perfect guest but so I wouldn't be alone, even though he didn't even know what company I typically kept. The proceedings at the hospital, in Clamart, happened on January 2. It was especially ominous.

Rachid was going back to Morocco at the end of his Christmas vacation and nobody knew when he'd be able to come back to France and, because I was a writer, he asked me for a book I'd written. I gave him the *Jim-Courage* book which was special for me because it had taken Michel's death for me to write this book all about Gérard, because Hervé had liked it so much and it was thanks to him that I'd met Bernardo. "I'd never have called you back if the book hadn't won me over like that," Rachid said many years later. When he managed to get back to Paris after I'd gone to see him several times in Morocco ("the visas, the visas," we'd say over the years the same way other folks would say "the contracts, the contracts"—each time, it was hell, without any of the humor in the Gaston Lagaffe comics), he was the lucky recipient, since he was such a fan of them and he had such different tastes from me when it came to clothes, of those Roman T-shirts from Emporio Armani that he was touched to learn had come to me, in a way, from Hervé despite not having a single compunction about tossing them when he had to whereas I would have kept them like relics until they were falling to pieces. That was so him, that was so me.

He saw a picture of me that he liked. I told him about it. I liked it, too, and I was generally uncomfortable with pictures. As there always has to be a public-use photo that the publisher gives the press when a book comes out, Hervé had suggested (or had I asked him?) to take this one for the publication of *Jim-Courage*. I was on the floor at his place and, in my opinion, I looked like I was twenty when I was actually thirty. I wanted to keep it forever as my press photo because I thought it was well-done and it would spare me a further sitting session. Over the years, the staff at Editions P.O.L hinted that I hadn't found the fountain of eternal youth and that at the very least current matters called for a replacement. I wrote *Jim-Courage* for Gérard and also, in my heart, for Michel, and it turned out that despite myself I'd also written it for Hervé and then for Bernardo and for Rachid. In the text was an outing I'd had with Valentin, a boy I'd met years earlier and who, as with Rachid, I'd fallen in love with immediately, but, in the book, it played out with Gérard because he was the protagonist. It took me time to realize how tactless I'd been with both Gérard and Valentin in this false attribution. But I was Hervé's reader, and I had to learn for myself where truth and reality ought not to meet.

The Villa pensionnaires could take a "study trip" during their stay. His second year, when we could both do it (it was once each year), Hervé took his in Italy with Eugène. Not for a minute was I considered. Once we'd gotten to know each other, he'd hoped that we'd go together to New York, but, deep down, I'd never been interested and I said no at some point before the very end. Thanks to *Le Monde* and *Le Nouvel Observateur* and *Libération*, our respective employers, we'd gone together to Avoriaz, Berlin and Naples, Bastia and Munich, but, just like when we'd spent time in Elba, those weren't trips, strictly speaking, we got there and we didn't venture much. Going from town to town, especially in a country where I didn't speak the language, was too anxiety-inducing, and that wasn't any more appealing to me than such a companion was to Hervé. He asked me to loan him a book I liked for the trip.

It was a Swiss book-club edition of two of Flaubert's earliest works, *Memoirs of a Madman* and *November*. I love those texts and the physical book—a tiny thing that fit in a shirt pocket and had been gifted to me by Denis, my Swiss friend from the *Minuit* magazine. There was no way I could refuse to lend it to Hervé but I gave him a hundred entreaties, to the effect that I really did care about this book and it would be impossible to find another copy and could he please do everything not to lose it. Of course he lost it. The second-to-last sentence in *November* had always struck me and reading it out loud to him was what convinced him to fall in love with it (as if Flaubert alone couldn't have done so): "Finally, last December, he died, but slowly, little by little, by mere dint of thinking, without any organ being affected, the way one dies of sadness—which will appear rather difficult to people who have suffered a great deal; but you have to put up with it in a novel, for love of the marvellous." Fortunately, I wouldn't have any love of such marvelousness outside literature. To assuage me, Hervé got me a copy of Gallimard's impossible-to-find Pléiade album about Proust which I'd spent ages looking for.

Was there some tactlessness in luring Hervé to this text with the sentence I read out loud? When it came to death, he was beyond any tact. What was actually shocking was that one day, when I was complaining to the Director, who hadn't noticed yet, about putting on weight, he said, "Who cares?"—since I already had Bernardo and this other Brazilian man I'd met in Rome. I kept that in mind and put on further weight without kicking up a fuss.

Hervé's sociability in the Villa changed between his first year and my second. At first, there was Alain and especially Eugène, although he did spend time with other pensionnaires as *Incognito* makes clear. When I came, the three of us—me, Hervé, Eugène—were always together. In the final year, I was certainly in Rome for a few stretches without him, even if I hardly remember it, but my relationship with Xavier (and not Patrick the writer) wouldn't have deepened had Hervé been a constant presence. I kept him up to date on everything, serving as a logbook of sorts, as if we were keeping track of minutiae at the Académie, or as if we were just concierges. My first year, one night, to avoid going to a restaurant, we decided to have dinner at the Salon des pensionnaires, as we could if we'd bought tickets and reserved seats before nine in the morning. That wasn't our way of doing things but we wanted to give it a try. It turned out to be four or five pensionnaires, us included, at a huge table with a white tablecloth, served as if at a dinner for thousands by uniformed *cameriere* we were on good terms with and who, here, stood to our left and presented us, as if we were dignitaries, dishes that hardly warranted such reverence. I thought of this meal—there was only one, we didn't go through that a second time—when, years later, a friend told me this story: Maurice Pialat, a guest at a fancy dinner at a big-shot producer's, was offered a dish by a white-gloved domestic and, noticing the gloves, said to the domestic: "Oh, do you have eczema too?"

There was a lunch, a barbecue of sorts on the grounds, to welcome the new pensionnaires, my second year, and I went. Hervé wasn't in Rome but he got to hear my recollection of it. Marie and Jean-Yves were there, as was a pensionnaire's boyfriend, a nice guy, but maybe a bit too friendly. He picked up some meat with his fingers while saying to Marie, "When in Africa," figuring that the darkness of her skin meant she ate without a fork. "Where were you born?" he asked her. "Pithiviers, France," she said, making me think of an investigation from the early days of the magazine *Gai-Pied* where Caribbean men were asked about how they were perceived in gay bars, and one of them said that he was always asked, "What are you?" which he answered with "I'm a guy." Another instance of casual racism: a few months later, Hervé was at some event since the pensionnaires had known the host would be doing something, and a couple of the guests there, amid the aforementioned scrum of kids, spoke to Marie as if she were their nanny. (When Rachid came to the Villa, there hadn't been very many Moroccan writers there before him.) Fortunately, Jean-Yves didn't overhear the conversation;

he was quick to snap at how people behaved toward Marie, accusing the Romans of racism for staring at her as if he didn't realize just how beautiful she was. He told me that he'd gotten into an argument with a pensionnaire who, noticing that I wasn't in Rome, said I had to be getting fucked in Paris backrooms. I was grateful to Jean-Yves but not angry at the pensionnaire. That just gave Hervé and me something to talk about, and there was a broadly reassuring backdrop to it all, a gaiety, a lightness that illness couldn't dent.

I don't recall ever having seen Hervé in a bed. Maybe that was another reason of his, or mine, for my never visiting him at the hospital. Even that night when I slept so badly in his apartment, I didn't see him between his sheets because he was sleeping on the mezzanine and I was at the back of the ground floor, just below, with the floor of his room as my ceiling. When he slept in my apartment, it was he who was on the lower floor and me above where the bathroom was, such that when we said good-night I went up and didn't have to come back down and, when I descended in the morning after my shower, he was already up and his bed made. (That final year, we also took break-fast together, on top of the other meals, but most often at the badly-stocked Villa bar where we didn't have to pay, no more than the drinks we offered each other over the course of the day, each of us pensionnaires having a tab that we paid at the end of the month and which we couldn't be entirely sure hadn't been padded out a bit but which we paid all the same.) And when he slept in my bed with Rodrigue (if that's what they were doing), I was considerate enough to wait until he came down before I went up. On every trip we took, when we stayed in hotels, it was rare for one of us to go into the other's room. Was it because I'd had sexual feelings for him? I no longer felt that way about him and maybe never had, for all his handsomeness he wasn't sufficiently my type to warrant mustering the courage to proposition him since it's always such a leap for me to take that step that I have to feel outright compelled to. Years before we were pensionnaires there, Hervé had been invited to the Villa by a pensionnaire who was a photographer and we'd both slept in a bedroom in the Palais. In the same bed? Probably. We'd skinny-dipped together on Elba but the other's bed, in one way or another, was a sanctuary of sorts, even if, when he started to give me his manuscripts or galley proofs to read or reread and over the course of this process which bound us together we went through my comments sitting side by side on my bed because my Paris apartment barely had enough space.

When he was a pensionnaire, Hervé's apartment was at the end of the path rightly called the Orange Trees. Just as it was beautiful by day, so it was sinister by night. If it hadn't been within the Villa, we'd have called it a death trap. Hervé asked for it to be lit up to no avail, but by the time Rachid was a pensionnaire, ten years later, when I visited the Académie then, his request had been fulfilled posthumously. Oddest was that this interminable path, as infinite in my memory as Michel's book was for Hervé, seemed far shorter than I'd ever recalled it being, the same way that rooms or things that seem so big as a child turn out to be very reasonably sized when confronted anew as an adult. But I wasn't a child when I was a pensionnaire. Or *were* we? Had the Villa reactivated this youth that had gone, and wholesale for Hervé, granting us such lightness in what could have been a leaden atmosphere, rendering us rascals with rascals' fears and worries, those worries doing their best to hold their own, to keep open their gaping maw in the light of a dread on a far greater scale.

After *Learning What Love Means* came out, readers, alluding to Michel and Hervé, often told me just how lucky I was to know such human beings. And, for a long time, I just nodded yes, what a wonderful thing that had been in my life, yes, how nice it'd been. Over time, it came to annoy me, something about the tone especially, as if it was luck alone that had created these friendships, as if anyone meeting one or the other could have been so close, that it was nothing to do with me myself. And, more than anything, as if they hadn't died. I wrote in *Learning What Love Means* that it was great luck to have met Michel but that greater than that was to have known him. The same, of course, goes for Hervé and for any beloved lost. But the natural flow of generations hadn't prepared me for seeing Hervé saddled with a fate so different from mine. Our playfulness early on had given way to a sort of start of a happy death where the roles, fortunately for me, couldn't have been more evenly split. It took me a good long while after his death to realize that I'd more or less lived with him in Rome, because, up until then, I'd had a different idea of what "live with" meant.

When I came to the Villa, Hervé knew everyone, Évelyne and Michelena but also the Director and his wife, the other members of the administration who each had a singular fondness for him, the staff members who were skilled at fixing things, the plumber, the electrician. As well as Saïd at the porter's house, there was a special love for Luigi, the Director's *cameriere* who was involved in all those Villa matters that were secondary for the pensionnaires but essential for the Italian folks who had a special status. There were more of them than there were lodgings meant for them in the park, so much more that those who didn't have access were very jealous, and, as they were parceled out according to rules connected to family lineages, there were times when a father would have to put forth superhuman efforts to make sure that, upon his death, his apartment would pass to his son, and sometimes the places fell into disrepair.

It was the pensionnaires that Hervé seemed to have the least connection with at first, whereas racking up keys to the most prestigious guest bedrooms, which he'd managed to get when one of his friends had stayed in this or that particular room, the Turkish bedroom, the Cardinal's bedroom, brought him all the glee of a pensionnaire as distracted as a schoolboy; he'd also snagged the one to the Director's elevator which let him reach those upper floors without wearing himself out. On the other side, the bedroom called the Tower, at the top of the Palais and overlooking Rome, had no such contraption because at the time it was assigned to a pensionnaire. The one who'd landed it was so proud of it, but going up and down those hundreds of steps was hellish, all the more so since the room was unbearably hot when the sun was pounding down and the view that was presumed to be magnificent felt lifeless because it was too high up, all the people looking, as they did for Orson Welles in the Ferris wheel in *The Third Man*, like ants and insects, and my own view, my second year, just above the roofs, seemed a thousand times more charming. And we had great fun joking about the others as if it was us who'd had the most right to be happy.

The Salon des pensionnaires was a place where people hung out in hopes of seeing someone when they really were bored (sometimes I went there alone, Hervé never did unless he had something to do there). It was adjacent to the bar and the library. The library itself was wonderful: a narrow space above the garden with views on both sides, it had heaps of books each with a borrowing card that showed who—whether famous or anonymous—had checked it out and that made it a pleasure to discover shared reading experiences. Hervé recalled all the silliness he'd indulged in with the French librarian and the Italian librarian since, with them, he'd forged particular friendships as well. I'm hard pressed to better describe or define this deep connection than to say that he'd succeeded.

My second year, some pensionnaires (on Xavier's initiative, either because that's the most likely thing or because that's what I recall), set up the ping-pong table right in front of the library door just so; if a player missed a serve right when the door had opened, the ball would go sailing into the library with that annoying noise that bouncing ping-pong balls make that could barely (but just barely) be heard through the shut door. It was a constant tug-of-war between the pensionnaires using their stay to get work done and those using it not to work. Despite myself, I was living proof that not working was taking full advantage of my time there, while Hervé was the proof of the converse. He was so happy at the Villa that he simply had to like me as well, that final year; otherwise he wouldn't have been there. The time for exasperation was past. The worse stages of his illness would be in Paris, upon his definitive return which my presence in Rome staved off.

Did he die in Rome? On the contrary, it was as if he would never die there. Defiance toward Italian hospitals was a constant among the pensionnaires. It was simple: Hervé almost never went to the hospital. He had no business there apart from blood draws, he had his French treatment which he polished off right there. He was in the state he was in, but Rome still meant vacation (a working one, in the best sense of the term), meant the Villa, meant its particular form of *la dolce vita*. He'd lived on his own terms, he'd die on his own terms. It would be great courage to live and it would be great courage to die and the two converged and the two diverged. He wanted to see it—his own death—he was set on front-row seats, it would have been ridiculous to have gone so thoroughly over his life only to let go of it as it stretched toward the farthest reaches. Neither Rome nor the Villa would have that effect; the time simply hadn't come. I don't know why I'm writing this paragraph, suddenly there's something of a novel there, but it's so striking that I have to concede it's struck a nerve.

How can anyone share a single death? Hervé felt some sort of remorse, even though it wasn't his fault, at being so much worse off than Thierry and Christine; the prospect never occurred to him that Thierry might not outlive him for long and that Christine would outlive him for a long, long while. He felt like he'd spoiled the already-horrible path ahead of them by going down it first and describing every painstaking detail as if they couldn't have anything of their own to discover and that itself would be yet another woe. He felt like he'd stolen something from them despite himself. He'd gotten both the worse part of the bargain because he was forging onward like a scout fully aware of his final destination and the better part of the bargain because it was a new thing he was exploring in the heart of this unknown that was an illness as a very long flight of steps to be walked alone and he was describing it so precisely that it was no longer an unknown for them, that they would only have to follow his lead which would be the least promising thing of all. In *To the Friend Who Did Not Save My Life*, he fought in hopes of a new treatment but this hope ended up being extinguished and all he could see for Thierry and Christine was the same fate he'd faced. He wasn't ready for everything but he was ready to try everything for the sake of his work. In the hospital, at the end, his sister, whom he'd reconnected with in his final months, was fixated on anything that would keep him alive in case a miracle treatment would appear, even as his being was proof that nothing could heal him now. But it was a matter of time: Hervé, on the contrary, didn't imagine that Christine would be saved.

Sharing his death with Thierry and Christine had already struck him as uneven despite their also being HIV-positive, so how could his death be shared with me as well? And what part could or should I play in all this? These illogical, obscene questions hung over us. He was living in the Villa in a cloistered world, because most of our time was spent within its walls, where each of us, whether pensionnaire or administrator or *cameriere*, knew that he and he alone would die (it wasn't like a hospital or a nursing home). At the end he wore that red hat that made him distinctive even at a distance, but he had been distinctive even at a distance before then. The hat led him to take charge again. Often, I wasn't sure how I should behave when it came to his death. Alluding to it, steeping myself in it, wasn't courageous, and I had no part to play in his own courage. I figured the best I could do was to keep up the silly or wise joy that had always been at the heart of our relationship, and maybe that wasn't such a bad idea. I tried to be there, too, when there was no place for pleasure, although I was less self-assured there. I knew how to go on living after losing a loved one, I didn't have to imagine it. Not everyone can be the hero of *November*.

At some point my Wikipedia page said that I'd gone with Hervé to the Villa and that felt wrong to me, by all rights it was Hervé who'd gone with me, the final year, when he wasn't a pensionnaire anymore but I still was. And yet. Two or three years after Hervé's death, René de Ceccatty published a book called *L'Accompagnement*. He recounted the death (by AIDS) of a writer friend I'd also known (we'd been lovers) and who'd foisted on him the responsibility of penning those final days, "this struggle against death in the hospital," when the dying man no longer had enough strength to write. *L'Accompagnement* was literary and yet no less concrete. It wasn't so stark for me; Hervé had described his decline with every last bit of strength he had left, apart from the final weeks in the hospital, where, as I understand, the doctors' courage paled in comparison to his (but I'm hardly the best judge of that). During his previous hospital stays, I'd never visited him because he hadn't explicitly asked for it, which made it all the more striking that he asked for me to come straightaway in his final phone call. At this point I can see that, facts aside, there would have been something presumptuous about saying that Hervé had gone with me to the Villa. As hazy as the details might seem, it was very much I who'd accompanied him. In his delight that I'd finally won the competition, when he was already at the Villa, there was some pleasure to be found for me, but also for him, I would be a friend in Rome, and for two new years. I'd more or less successfully gone with him and it was by far the most important thing I did in Rome where I didn't write a thing.

The Villa's always stirred up or created its fair share of drama. I've mentioned the pensionnaire's companion who, having given birth, tried to throw her baby out of a window. The Secretary General proved himself in the same mindset as Hervé and me by saying "How can anyone be depressed in such a pretty place?" In *Incognito* there's a murder and the Italian police try to blame it on a pensionnaire (and that wasn't just a figment of Hervé's imagination). Just as I alluded to an architect pensionnaire who was a bit of a medieval lord, so there was a more sympathetic pensionnaire to whom Xavier had, upon leaving, sold the scooter that he'd used so he wouldn't wear himself out walking in the garden or going up a single step from the Piazza di Spagna—and Xavier had sold it at a ridiculously inflated price which he took great pleasure in telling me about. Twenty years after leaving the Villa, this architect killed his wife who wanted to divorce him while his daughters and a friend of theirs were downstairs. If he ever gets out of prison, he'll be an old man. That little scandal was the talk of the town and, when I told Rachid and an old pensionnaire friend of his that I'd known that architect and been friends with him, the friend had been stunned, saying that one really has to wonder where people who do those sorts of things come from and, look, there was an answer for this one! Hervé was a walking death in the Villa. He had nothing to do there, death was there, for him and with him and in him, the way government is said to be of the people and by the people and for the people. Death was there, there was no theorizing it or solving it. Dying in my apartment, if that did happen, would have been, in the administration's eyes, one last trick Hervé had played on them. But, in Rome, he wasn't that far gone. And AIDS hadn't decimated my entourage at that point, back then funerals were still a rare thing for me.

I'm mixing up my stays as if there'd only been a long one broken into various parts, which isn't entirely wrong. I'm recounting this as if all we did were silly things, but that's not so; we might have been real pieces of work, but more often we were kind, I think, and not only to one another; as if on one side was life and on the other death, sickness facing off against health, but not entirely. Our relationship wasn't all that different in Rome from in Paris: our earlier closeness had been brought to Rome, and our Roman closeness flourished in Paris, in this stretch where we were torn between two cities. But, in Paris, we were never getting on each other's nerves, even when we saw each other constantly, we could choose not to. When all is said and done, even in Rome Hervé was never a burden for me, on the contrary (nor was I for him, in the long run, paradoxically): I declared that, considering that, when his lover Rodrigue was present, our tête-à-têtes being interrupted suddenly seemed less of a bother to me than other prospects might be. All the pensionnaires in my second year and their partners, when they talked about Hervé, said *Hervé* so naturally: he was there, right there. Maybe I'm mixing up the stays but I'm sure I haven't done so with his presence.

To the Friend Who Did Not Save My Life stirred up some sort of pure admiration in me. It was his death that he was starting to write after having written his life so well and I was like a child, all lost in my goodwill, some sort of belief in magic, as if he could have written such a book and it would have all been lies, that all that would remain would be the text's literary quality while Hervé would in fact not have been infected, that nothing but long years lay ahead for him and for us both. At my father's funeral, there had been his sister and his two brothers, one of whom had been sick for years, while the way my father had been borne away was far more sudden. And my healthy uncle, when his brother passed away, said: "Who'd have guessed that Laurent would outlive Jérôme?" It was ten years after Hervé's death but I had thoughts like that back then. I was just believing that anything could happen—but in the wrong way. Hervé might have outlived me too, since I could have been hit by a car or laid low by an even worse illness. In the end, Hervé wanted to die, all his friends and family kept telling me that, and that was what he'd conveyed when he'd called me that last time. But even then he had to fight. There wasn't this abyss that all opponents of euthanasia fall into, the divide between the dying man's wishes and those of the ones who love him. Everything aligned. And yet, as close as we might be, why are we so far from one other when one of us dies? And how can that distance change, grow and shrink over the years after?

We almost never talked about our childhood. Our respective adventures as teens were mysteries to ourselves. For all we knew about each other's present-day love lives (in any case mine for him), I was wholly ignorant of Hervé's before we met. How wise I'd been at the outset of our friendship, figuring that he'd had years of debauchery, unbridled sexuality, a thousand experiences involving every sort of drug! I'd never learned the facts about a single aspect ("I'm not an easy guy," he said all the same right after our meeting when I realized that he probably was) but I'd come to gain a substantial wealth of experience in drugs that he'd never had, even if the ease with which he accepted me in one state or another could only mean a familiarity implying knowledge or habit, albeit temporary. *Propaganda Death* revealed such an unusual relationship with the body that this body had to have undergone unusual adventures, if only in an imagination that was already outsize and all the more so in broad daylight. The back-cover text of the first edition of that book, which was the first one of his that I read shortly after meeting him, went: "*Propaganda Death* is the account of an act of love that does not culminate in climax but continues into murder, death, and beyond. It's the murderous body and the murdered body in conversation as they commingle." (Reusing this first title as the headline announcing his death was a very wise choice on *Libération*'s part.)

My admiration for *My Parents*, the shock that reading the book resulted in was as much due to the excerpt Hervé had published in the magazine *Masques*, where he described his first love, dwelled on the funnel chest that he hated and that I knew well because he never stopped hating it even if he had less compunction about letting it be seen and that apparently perfectly fit a protrusion on another's chest. This extract was titled "The Highest, Blondest Lock of Hair" and I'd made fun of Hervé because of the sentimental aspect of this title. I really couldn't get over it when I saw just how violent the whole manuscript was, and how truly unsentimental it was. But there was also, in this lock of hair, Hervé's relationship with his hair. He mentions in *To the Friend Who Did Not Save My Life* the shock he'd given Michel when one day he'd shown up with his ringlets chopped off, and that Muzil had to catch his breath. I don't recall being surprised at all the first time I saw Hervé transformed thus. I'm not sure I even realized it. It wasn't "Hervé bobs his hair" à la the F. Scott Fitzgerald story. My father was bald like his father before him, and, like Hervé, I was scared of the same happening to me. But that was purely theoretical, I didn't dwell on it daily, just as Hervé's physique could have seemed abstract to me when I fell in love with it the first time we met. He was handsome, that was plain as day, and my body didn't insist on particulars. There was no hurt, no bitterness in my not ever sleeping with him, thanks to his attentiveness and his thoughtfulness, but also because our friendship was fulfillment enough for me as it must have been for him; as I've already said, sexuality for me was more a means than an end, and without it I'd never have gone to the trouble to get to know him so well. In my typical idiocy, it took me ages to notice his physical degradation—so why would I blink twice at his haircuts? I have no memory of him going to the barber's in Rome (I never did), not of him telling me about it, not of me noticing it. He was Hervé, his beauty was fully assumed, and, deep down, it was all the same to me because it was Hervé. He had his own way of doing things, and why shouldn't being beautiful be included?

In Paris, it was rare for one of us to go to the other's place. My first year in Rome, not a day went by that it didn't happen. We picked each other up, we accompanied each other, we didn't stop, it was a pleasure to knock at the door and go in. It wasn't our apartment properly speaking, just the lodgings assigned to us, but even so . . . The second year, he stayed at my place, because administratively it remained my place, even if Hervé had managed to dig up in some storage space or another of the Villa's where he knew that a few paintings could be borrowed to spruce up the place, one of which was a little Jacques-Louis David that wasn't a David but a reproduction made by a pensionnaire and that I was delighted to see again in one of his photos. It was my place because I could be there without him and he couldn't always without me, a proof of sorts of his erasure, this fate that was a goal for Michel at the end of his life and that was weighing on Hervé, on the contrary happy to display his weakened body with a sort of militant exhibitionism that was courage, because this militancy wasn't for an established cause but created one that I was hard-pressed to define, attached to illness and literature and life and death and each person's personal identity, unshareable yet shared by literature. I had every reason to be proud that he was at my place, that everything had come together so that he could continue his work, so that his life and his death could unite there because he had no other choice on that front. It was my place but I was happy and proud when it was *our* place.

To write about Rome is to pass over everything I don't dare to write about because it's too complicated to lay a claim to Hervé and writing always amounts to that. To write about Rome is to write about what came after the exasperation that he was able to express in his exasperated text, when our shared peace stood out. It's to write about what he didn't write, not to risk competing with it. Because it would be odd to find Hervé in someone else's book, he who is so thoroughly in his own, even if that someone else were me. That's pointless, I'm happy to write but I don't feel any need to. I can see him walking, I can hear him talking, there's no point writing it. I can't see or hear him so clearly anymore and I'm unable to share him, description isn't enough. 268: his apartment number in the Villa phone book comes back to me, I'd dialed it countless times each day almost to the exclusion of all the others. Just picking it up when it rang was enough to make us laugh, there was no question that it'd be the other one at the other end of the line in those days when numbers didn't appear on a screen, especially not in the Villa where nothing worked well, where we always had to unplug this and plug in that before we could turn on the television in the Salon des pensionnaires. To write about Rome is to write about a time when I knew that words always referred to an eternity so fleeting that there was no reason to use them or even think them. It's to write about a time when I wasn't the one threatened by death, when through some magical yet unremarkable phenomenon it was relegated elsewhere, not overtly threatening me.

I tell Claire about this text and she's amazed that I'd wax poetic about Rome ("what a silly idea"). I met her almost upon meeting Hervé because she was his best friend at *Le Monde*. I've kept her up to date with my project from the outset, when it was just a matter of bequeathing my inscribed copies of Hervé's books to the IMEC, and she didn't think it was such a great idea to go bury them there with my comments that nobody would read. I've decided that I'm appending Hervé's inscriptions over the years, and any explanation I can furnish of what of our relationship can be recounted, to this book. She listens to me without any response.

Suddenly I realize just how cookie-cutter researchers interested in Hervé will be. It's not for them that I want to make his inscriptions and my comments available, and yet I'm happy that they'll be able to take advantage of it. Why, then? I don't know. To describe a relationship, convey an idea of friendship, which someone will always be researching. To get around my inability. To write about my connection with Hervé, from start to finish and from A to Z. I feel like I can't pull it off myself, it's an impossible task that gives me no pleasure to tackle, it's too much for me, and even its very terms would be practically beyond me. I don't want to do it, that's a good enough reason for not doing it even if just writing is often a way to write exactly what I don't want to write and vice-versa; for example, before I finish, maybe I should touch lightly on some fond memory, which might be both nonchalant and as touching as can be, minimalism for maximum effect. Well, sometimes, that's literature. And sometimes I miss Hervé because I'd like to show him what I'm writing, see what he thinks. Certainly that won't be happening for this text—and yet . . .

What more can I say? "Hervelino, Hervelino," I sometimes say out loud, when I'm alone at home, when I'm thinking about Hervé.

Suzanne et Louise, 1980.

Pour mon copain Mathieu
pour les flaques, pour les crétins
pour qu'on parle de toi
pour notre bêtise si joyeuse
pour l'Irish Coffee du Bonaparte
les flipers du Tabac des Sports
pour Avoriaz
un cuistre, un crétin ridicule
vraiment pitoyable
qui n'a jamais aimé aucun homme
ni aucune femme
pour la nuit du Chasseur,
pour Forêts (ils sont de bonne
connivence ces deux. là)
pour le voyage aux États-Unis,
et qu'il ne finisse pas à Chambéry,
bref pour tous ces bons souvenirs
et toutes ces bonnes blagues,
et qu'il y en ait encore beaucoup
d'autres...

Mathieu je t'embrasse

hervé.

For my friend Mathieu
for the puddles, for the idiots
for talking about you
for our very silly fun
for Irish coffee at Bonaparte
the pinball machines at the Tabac des Sports
for Avoriaz
an oaf, a ridiculous idiot
utterly pitiful
who never liked a single man
or woman
for night of the hunter,
for Forêts (those two really are in cahoots)
for the USA trip,
for it not ending up in Chambéry,
—for all these great memories
and all these great jokes,
and to many, many, many more …
for Mathieu with love
hervé.

I've described how Michel Foucault had Hervé and me meet in summer 1978, and how, from the end of that year, once I was over my crush, we became friends. We spent plenty of evenings together, just the two of us at his place or mine, living as friends, having dinner then hanging out at bars. It's those evenings that the puddles, the idiots, our silly fun, café Bonaparte, the Tabac des Sports, the oafs, and the stupid idiots are referring to. Also, I made Hervé go see *The Night of the Hunter* (a cult film at the time) and "Forests" is one of my texts that he read at my place after I'd clumsily burned it, the singed sheets in his hand only made him appreciate these survivors even more.

Avoriaz is a resort in the Alps that held a fantasy-film festival where we spent five days in winter 1980, him for *Le Monde* and me for *Le Nouvel Observateur*, the previous iteration of *L'Obs*. It was as if more people had been shipped over from Paris than lived in Avoriaz and they'd become the actual inhabitants of the city, a bad mix of pitiful snobbishness and far too much money. That was our first trip together, we were ill at ease even though we had all our meals together, and going through this ordeal of a festival where we laughed constantly only brought us closer together.

"Pitiful": we'd had dinner at Hervé's, in his studio on rue de Vaugirard where we must not have had any other dinners, with Michel Foucault, his friend Daniel and my friend Thierry, thanks to whom I'd met Michel, and who'd brought the first issue of *Gai Pied*, a brand-new monthly gay magazine which Michel had given a text to via Thierry and which—he didn't learn until he saw the cover—had had a terrible title slapped on it, which immediately resulted in so much awkwardness that he just as immediately tried to clear up. But it was palpable and when Hervé told me over the phone the next day that the evening had been pitiful, I'd just tried to please him by saying yes like an idiot, which made him laugh and then made me laugh too and so that adjective stuck with us.

I'd used the phrase "who never liked a single man or woman" in an article and Hervé had been delighted that I would put those genders rejected by a novel's narrator in that order. It was a review of the book *Mars*, by a Swiss man using the pseudonym Fritz Zorn, where he talked about how the cancer killing him was the fulfillment of his life, of the way he'd led it. When *To the Friend Who Did Not Save My Life* came out, reviewers mentioned *Mars*.

He suggested that we go to New York together in the summer of 1980. But I was hardly a traveler before my lovers' moves forced me to be (he went without me). Back then, Paris was covered with posters for a new airline with the slogan "All airlines don't go to Chambéry. Ours do." And I made Hervé laugh by piping up with an anxious-sounding voice every time we came across one of those posters: "Oh, isn't it lucky that all airlines don't go to Chambéry. Just imagine us boarding for Stockholm or Mexico and always landing in Chambéry."

Ghost Image, 1981.

Mathieu
i want to write you an inscription so sweet that I'm
afraid of never living up to it. In any case I'm sending
you my love, as much as usual, and I won't forget your
kindness in helping me revise this book:
                                        hervé july 23 '81.

It was a few months before I met Hervé that
Propaganda Death came out, and *Suzanne et Louise* is com-
posed of photos and handwritten texts that, too, were
photographed; *Ghost Image*, consequently, is the first book
of his that I read before publication (in manuscript and

proof form), telling Hervé who'd asked me about my suggestions. That would become a gimmick in our relationship. He would come over to my place, we would sit down side by side on my bed and I would saddle him with all the comments I'd made in pencil so that he could do as he saw fit with them. He thought I was perfectly capable, which was my opinion as well, but years later I was able to do the same thing with a filmmaker friend, leaning that time on my being perfectly incapable, which granted us the same freedom, on my end to say whatever I thought when I came out of the screening and on his to use it or not.

It's also the first book of Hervé's to have come out from Éditions de Minuit—at the time run by my father—after all the texts he'd published in the *Minuit* magazine, which Denis Jampen and I were running.

*Once I'd met Hervé, owing to the genuine feeling I had for him, I got a copy of *Propaganda Death* and shared my impressions with him, specifically a critique I can't remember anymore of the book's composition. As I did so, the possibility that being so forthright, which I deemed necessary, as if Hervé's total involvement with literature meant that he couldn't be put off by being confronted with the truth (which my opinion would have amounted to), might be a strategic blunder, never occurred to me. And, indeed, it brought the two of us closer together.

Singular Adventures, 1982.

Mathieu
the feeling I have for you, and which has only grown
in the time I've known you, is one of my greatest com-
forts, I hope you can tell . . .
This "dedication" is my chance to tell you that, and to
send you, once again, all my love:
hervé
(March 28, 1982)

Les Chiens, 1982.

In its manuscript, it was a single volume: *Les Chiens*—
"The Dogs"—was the last of the *Singular Adventures*. My
father wanted to separate that text from the rest owing to
its erotic or pornographic nature—I think he presumed
this aspect might tinge the whole collection and draw
attention to that one text. Hervé was delighted by this
proposal which he immediately accepted.

The two books came out at the same time and, in my
head, Hervé only ever inscribed *Les Chiens* with this heart
but I don't know where I got that idea.

Voyage avec deux enfants, 1982.

Pour Mathieu,
bien sûr présent dans
l'irruption sentimentale
de ce livre (mais tu auras
remarqué qu'il n'y a pas
de valeur d'attachement dans
l'ordre d'apparition...), et encore

VOYAGE
AVEC DEUX ENFANTS

présent au moment de ses
épreuves, pour me soutenir de
ses précieux conseils.
Que ce livre soit l'occasion,
polisson, de te redire une
fois de plus combien je t'aime :
hervé
(à Rio Elba, où nous avons
passé ensemble ces jours de
charme antique et à la tortue...
le 2 août 1982)

For Mathieu,
of course present in this book's sentimental upwelling
(but it'll be obvious that emotional weight doesn't
factor into the order of appearance . . .), and still
present at the time of its proofs, to support me with his
valuable advice.
may this book be the opportunity, rapscallion, to
remind you one more time just how much i love you:
hervé
(at Rio Elba, where we spent those days hunting the
tiger and the turtle together . . .
august 2, 1982).

I think 1982 was my first stay on Elba, that place
Hervé loved going to and where his friend Hans-Georg
had two places to welcome him: the Santa Caterina hermitage, where Hervé hoped in vain to be buried, and his
house in the village. That time it was the three of us, I
think, in the hermitage (which was spartan), and the tiger
and turtle hunt turned out not to be a hunt, because the
cruising was at an absolute minimum, but an attentive,
watchful observation of two Rio Elba boys whose physical
or psychological characteristics assessed before I'd come
had granted them the nicknames of Turtle and Tiger; the
latter name was used for a character in *Blindsight*.

Regarding the "sentimental upwelling" of this book,
Michel Foucault, after reading it, said with his good smile
that he'd supposedly been furious at being hoodwinked by

thinking that it would be the one who'd been presented as the pretty boy that Hervé would fall in love with whereas, "of course," it could only be the one who'd been introduced as "the disgraceful boy."

*For a few weeks I'd hosted a literary show on Radio 7, the public service radio station for children before free radio. I'm such a stickler for journalistic integrity but I was so sure that not a single listener would ever buy a book that I felt no compunction about doing whatever I liked, for example, bringing on my friend Hervé for the release of his *Voyage*. "What's an 'enfant" to you, Hervé Guibert?" was the first question I asked him, because the book's protagonists struck me as far past the age of being called a child, and this question delighted us for quite a while, especially because the addition of his first and last name at the end was an echo of the first time I'd met him.

Arthur's Whims, 1983.

Mon loup

Ce livre t'est dédié para que je ne l'aurais jamais écrit* si je ne t'avais pas connu - et si je n'avais pas lu "Nos plaisirs"-, parce que j'avais hâte de te dédier un livre, parce que Lady Bigoudi est une pâle cousine de Mademoiselle Robin, et Bichon un frère de Serge-Lapin.

Bichon qui, comme toi, a des grains de beauté sur les omoplates- Tes adorables omoplates que j'embrasse :

A Mathieu.

Hervé
(le 25 septembre 1983)

(Et qui donc détient l'original de cette dédicace compromettante - pas assez à ton gré je suppose -, égarée maladroitement pour cause de fièvre au moment de sa rédaction le 9 septembre ? Qui sinon la reine des naines et des aspirateurs, des boiteuses, des couvertures chauffantes, des lampadaires, du Kung-fu, de l'épilation faciale, de la dinde surgelée, des fiascos, du poker, des cochonnes, des repasseuses, des lécheuses, des pilotes, des insuffisantes, des boîtes, des torquées, de la publicité, des taches, du fou-rire

ce livre n'aurait jamais existé
* si tu n'avais pas existé et si plus vraisemblablement ni je ne t'avais pas rencontré.

My wolf

this book is dedicated to you because I'd never have written it* if i hadn't known you—and if I hadn't read "Nos plaisirs"—because I couldn't wait to dedicate a book to you, because Lady Curlers is a pale cousin of Mademoiselle Robica, and Bichon a brother to Serge-Lapin.

Bichon who, like you, has beauty spots on his shoulders—your adorable shoulder blades which I love:

hervé

(September 25, 1983)

(And who hereby possesses the original of this compromising inscription—not sufficiently at your discretion I suppose—awkwardly lost on account of fever upon its composition on September 9? Who will be the queen of dwarves and vacuums, of gimps, of electric blankets, of streetlights, of Kung-fu, of facial-hair removal, of frozen turkey, of fiascos, of poker, of hussies, of ironers, of posers, of the sickly, of the insufficient, of cans, of madwomen, of ads, of stains, of giggles

*this book never would have existed if you hadn't existed and if more likely if I hadn't met you

Arthur's Whims is Hervé's only book to be dedicated to me in print. Mademoiselle Robica is a terrible character in my first novel, *Nos plaisirs*, and Serge-Lapin a darling in my second, *Prince et Léonardours.* Our swims on Elba were where Hervé noticed my speckled shoulder blades.

The parenthetical following the signature comes from the nickname the two of us had for Marguerite Duras: "the queen of queens and kings." Did she call herself that one day, maybe in a conversation? My guess is that Hervé'd actually thought up the line and it'd made me smile enough for us to keep it and that, on September 25, 1983, re-inscribing a copy that he'd given me in person after I'd lost the first one, he'd had great fun with those dreams and inanities we'd reveled in and I was proud to be the recipient whose presence ensured they wouldn't be lost.

I especially like that there's one "if" too many in what follows his asterisk; it's a correction that results in another correction.

Le Seul visage, 1984.

> *A mon plus lamentable*
> *modèle, mais non le*
> *moins aimé...*
> *A toi Mathieu : hervé*

LE SEUL VISAGE

To my most lamentable model, but not the least loved one . . .
To you Mathieu: hervé

I'm the most lamentable model because I'm incapable of posing for a photo, it makes me uncomfortable straightaway, I fidget and I don't know how to hold my body.

The photo on page 40, titled "Berlin-Est," was taken under the following circumstances. We were both on assignment in Berlin for the film festival, Hervé for *Le Monde* and me for *Le Nouvel Observateur*. It was in 1982, Fassbinder's *Veronika Voss* won the Golden Bear. Hervé was already familiar with the city and suggested that we skip a day of the festival to visit East Berlin where he wanted to go to a tearoom as gay as it was possible to be at that time in that part of town. We went, the tearoom was as empty as the bathroom of some floor I can't remember of some West Berlin department store I can't remember that he'd been told was a cruising spot, to be clear it was so deserted that after having come with high hopes we'd ended up giggling nonstop. As soon as we'd arrived, Hervé took me determinedly up the stairs to some floor I can't remember of some building I can't remember where we went into a room where I was totally disoriented and scared by the sounds I was hearing: it was an institution for the deaf and mute, and he hadn't warned me. When I read Hervé's fictionalization of this little jaunt, I told Michel Foucault that it was all wrong, it hadn't happened like that, and he responded by saying of Hervé: "Only false things happen to him," a line I liked so much that I'd parroted it to Hervé who'd liked it enough to refashion it in *To the Friend Who Did Not Save My Life.*

We'd left West Berlin very early and it was still early when we were walking down Unter den Linden. A little boy was hanging around there and with a few smiles we'd struck up a rapport. He didn't speak a word of French or English but he was so excited to meet strangers. Hervé was able to manage in German. There wasn't any discussion, but at that point he went with us like a guide, all smiles and full of joy and charm, taking us wherever he wanted, showing us whatever he wanted. We invited him to lunch (it might have been just a sandwich or a snack) then the rest of the afternoon was the same, he was comfortable with us and we with him. There was something odd and natural, we'd set out as a pair and ended up a trio, well, that was that. It was February, night was falling quickly, and Westerners would leave East Berlin just as they'd come, by taking the subway, a simple thing that wasn't so simple for East Berliners because that was where the checkpoints were. The little boy whose name I've forgotten went with us to the station and came down with us to the platform to wait for the train to come. We still made a natural trio. The subway came into the station and we got in. The doors shut. We'd barely said goodbye to him and then everything happened quickly all of a sudden. It was clear that we'd never see each other again. And, on an impulse, Hervé pulled out his camera and snapped a picture of him through the subway window. No photo of Hervé's touches me as much as this one.

Blindsight, 1985.

To you, Mathieu,
my wolf:
hervé
march 22, 1985

Blindsight is the first book Hervé published with Gallimard, after his dust-up with my father, a dust-up that had no effect on our friendship (or mine with my father).

My Parents, 1986.

et toc.

à mon ami Mathieu

grâce à qui la haine n'est pas
tendre, grâce à qui un exemplaire
de Bibi Fricotin ne coûte pas 150 F
pièce - ouf! -, grâce à toutes ces petites
catastrophes que tu m'as évitées pour
ce livre qui est une grande catastrophe
- ce livre qui, par un effet de
ton ignominieuse indulgence serait ton
préféré, à mon ami Mathieu enfin
grâce à la longue duquel mes fesses
sont propres tous les soirs depuis que
maman disparue ne veut plus s'en
occuper.

un gros baiser à mon Mathieu
de ton Hervelino penaud.

le 20 mars 1986

so there.

to my friend Mathieu

thanks to whom the hate is not tender, thanks to whom a copy of Bibi Fricotin doesn't cost 150 F—whew!—thanks to all these little catastrophes that you've saved me from for this book which is a huge catastrophe—this book which, by consequence of your ignominious indulgence, will be your favorite, to my friend Mathieu finally thanks to whose tongue my butt is clean each night ever since dearly departed mama didn't want to do it anymore.

a big kiss to my Mathieu from your hanged Hervelino.

March 20, 1986

"So there": I loved this text the very first time I read it and was blown away by its violence. Then when Hervé told me, months later, just before publication, that he was thinking about putting the line "Tender is the hate" on the belly band around the book, I'd been furious like it was a betrayal, like he was trying to patch things up. And because my fury was mock, I told him that, on the contrary, it seemed more appropriate to put on the belly band, if there was to be a belly band, "So there!" to add just a little something.

I think I'd made some pointless clarifications about the price of *Bibi Fricotin* when it came up.

My "ignominious indulgence" refers to a story that

was already an old story back then, because it was from 1982, during the FIFA World Cup. We'd both agreed to play a little role (two Indians, bare-chested and maybe just in underwear) in my friend Alain Fleischer's film—he was adapting Pierre Klossowski's *Roberte ce soir*. It had to do with a pilot, a few minutes that would help him get funding for the whole film. We did the shoot with Pierre and Denise Klossowski present. As Indians, we popped up out of nowhere and ran across the frame while whooping. It was all a lot of fun. But we had a meeting with Alain that Sunday afternoon, I was annoyed about the timing because it was right when France's soccer team was playing (against Czechoslovakia, I think, but maybe it was Kuwait) and Alain didn't show up, he was late, he was incredibly late, which drove me crazy because if I'd known I could have watched the game. And Hervé calmed me down with an indulgence that wasn't usually his strength and that only made me even more furious when I started thinking it was because he didn't care about the game. I snapped at him about his "ignominious virtue," a little quip that stuck with us for years.

Whatever one's thoughts about his butt, it in this case is a convenient way to segue to "dearly departed mama." *La Disparition de maman* is a 1982 book by Eugène Savitzkaya and an admiration for his books and an affection for the author were also things the two of us shared.

Hanging was a prospect that each of us envisioned for ourselves, enough that we mentioned it casually.

"*Pends-toi, Bill!*"—literally, "Hang yourself, Bill!"—is the third-to-last sentence in *To the Friend Who Did Not Save My Life*, and, for a while, was its title.

Vous m'avez fait former des fantômes, 1987.

à Mathieu,
qui m'a fait déborder
d'amour :
hervé

Vous m'avez fait déborder
d'amour
pour Mathieu Lindon
qui est un sale sadique
qui me torture depuis 1978
et j'en souffre beaucoup
mais comme je l'aime
j'accepte ma souffrance
Ta victime qui t'aime
et qui souffre et ne se plaint pas:
hervé

to Mathieu,
who's made me overflow with love:
hervé

You've made me overflow with love
for Mathieu Lindon
who's a filthy sadist
who's tortured me since 1978
and I suffer it so much
but as I love him
I accept my suffering
Your victim who loves you
and who suffers and does not complain:
hervé

I have two copies because the one sent through the mail must have gotten stuck and I'd figured it was lost, so Hervé had given me another one himself. We had a game going with his titles that I'll explain with *The Gangsters* and which explains the "You've made me overflow with love" for this novel.

At some point I highlighted the particular stretches of his conversation that struck me as awfully woeful, just so Hervé could have fun pretending to push back.

The Gangsters, 1988.

à Mateovitch,
amour de ma vie,
ma petite sardine rose,
l'inventeur d'Hervé Guibert,
réquisitionné pour tous les
soins d'urgence, jaloux des
broches que j'offre aux autres,
mais qui a perdu son petit chat,
mon loup adoré, combien de fois
assis sur ton lit nous avons
revu manuscrits, puis épreuves,
moi torturé et éperdu de
reconnaissance, voici donc la
très sensationnelle histoire des
Brigands, qui éclipse celle des
Chapeaux, en attendant Rouge la bite.
Je t'étouffe de baisers :
     ton hervelino que tu aimes plus
                              que tout

to Mateovitch,
love of my life,
my little pink sardine,
the inventor of Hervé Guibert,
requisitioned for all emergency treatments, jealous of
the pins I give others, but who lost his little cat,
my beloved wolf, how many times seated on your bed
did we go over manuscripts, then proofs, I tortured and
mad with gratitude, here is the very sensational story of
the Bandits, which eclipses that of the Hats ahead of
Red the Dick.
I smother you with kisses:
your hervelino who you love more than anyone

I no longer remember where exactly the expression "the inventor of Hervé Guibert" came from while "requisitioned for all emergency treatments" has to do with the body of the text, the disaster that was his great-aunts' affair and Hervé's shingles which nobody realized was a sign of his AIDS.

"Jealous of the pins . . ." At the time, pin-back buttons and campaign buttons were all the rage. Since Hervé gave them out to all his friends, I must have been amazed that I hadn't gotten one. So he gave me a little cat that I lost straightaway.

The Bandits, the Hats, Red the Dick: Hervé was always talking to me about his books here and there, so we were in the habit of my giving them a provisional, secret title (I say *my* because Hervé eventually turned his nose up and corrected an attempt that had fallen flat), so that we could talk about them without other people suspecting a thing. It was all in fun since we only ever talked about them when we were alone, apart from the staff at restaurants who we had no reason to think would care about our conversations. And so *The Gangsters* simply became "The Bandits" whereas *Vous m'avez fait former des fantômes*—"You've made me have dreams"—followed the principle of the infinitive structure and went through ridiculous avatars meant to offset the less ridiculous aspect of the book ("You've made me miss my train," "You've made me rip my pants," "you've made me eat steak," "You've made me go haywire") before settling on "You've made me twist my hats" and then its condensation, "the hats," which Hervé uses here. *Mauve the Virgin* had undergone a word-for-word transformation from *Mauve le vierge*, as if Mauve weren't the name of a person but a mere color, and *vierge* losing its *i* to become a word for penis, leading us to "Red the Dick" which was perfect for leading astray any potential exegete sent by foreign bodies to obtain confidential information about the short-story collection.

Mauve the Virgin, 1988.

à mon loup adoré,
Mathieu, ma bite rouge,
mon cul mauve, mon
maître et mon esclave,
mon mari, ma femme,
mon biniou, mon nalesniki,
ma Bernardina, mon
petit lapin romain :
hervé

to my beloved wolf,
Mathieu, my red dick,
my mauve ass,
my master and my slave,
my husband, my wife,
my tooter, my nalesniki,
my Bernardina, my little Roman rabbit:
hervé

I'm the little Roman rabbit because, if Hervé's been at
the Villa Médicis for a year, in fall 1988 I've just arrived

and we have the prospect of spending a year (in fact, two) together. Bernardina is a riff on Bernardino, the nickname I gave my Brazilian friend Bernardo (and which I dropped once he'd explained how utterly ludicrous it sounded in Portuguese). "Nalesniki," which is a plural that never should have been treated as a singular noun, is the name of the crêpes we had for dessert in a Russian restaurant on rue de Lappe that was called La Tchaïka (in English, "The Seagull," like Chekhov's play). I lived in the neighborhood, had walked past that restaurant ever since it'd opened and wanted to go in. It was a magnificent space in terms of its décor, ambiance, and cuisine, the only place we went on my own initiative, and we had countless dinners there.

Incognito, 1989.

Mathieu,
tu avais bien raison :
ce livre est médiocre et
vulgaire, nullard, anti-
pathique. Mais ^{toi} je t'aime
et je t'embrasse : hervé

Mathieu,
you were absolutely right: this book is mediocre and
vulgar, stupid, unpleasant. But I love you and I
send you my love: hervé

Despite the "you were absolutely right," I never used
any of those adjectives against *Incognito*—after reading
this inscription, just to play along, I'd protested, "Come
to think of it, didn't I say 'Frenchie'?" (a word that, of
course, I hadn't said either)—and this book's secret title
was "The Provisional Offenbach"; "Offenbach" owing to
the incognito quality of *La Périchole* and "provisional"
owing to the hopes we had of finding something better.
Hervé had dangled this book in front of me, saying that

I'd be bent over laughing, and I'd been let down. Hervé insisted that he didn't have much fondness for this book because of me but, when I read it years later, I liked it.

Crazy about Vincent, 1989.

> *to Mathieu,*
> *my love:*
> *hervé*
> *(Rome, August 7, 1989)*

The secret title of *Crazy about Vincent* was basically the initials of its French title, *Fou de Vincent*: "F2V." We liked that owing to its feeling of a secret code for an airplane prototype or some cartoon invention.

(On the same notebook page where I'd later found some Collected Poems was a phone number that was clearly Vincent's because Hervé wrote under it: "*V* who I'm not *F* about anymore."

To the Friend Who Did Not Save My Life, 1990.

à Mathieu mon petit chéri,
mon loup, mon amour, que
je n'ai pas cessé d'aimer de
plus en plus, et qui me l'a
bien rendu !
Je t'aime Mathieu, je
n'ai maintenant plus rien
d'autre à te dire dans une
dédicace.
Je t'aime de tout mon
cœur :

hervé

le 22 février 1990

to Mathieu my little darling, my wolf, my love, whom
I've only ever loved more and more, and who's done
likewise for me!
I love you Mathieu, now I don't have anything else to
tell you in an inscription.
I love you with all my heart:
hervé
February 22, 1990

Hervé must have thought this would be the last inscription he'd have the chance to write for me.

The Compassion Protocol, 1991.

LE PROTOCOLE COMPASSIONNEL

à Mathieu, l'amour de
ma vie, que j'aime plus
que tout, à mon loup
adoré, le génie modeste,
mon lapin chéri, à qui je
fais toujours, et pour cause,
les mêmes dédicaces depuis
13 ans !

Bisou :

hervé

to Mathieu, the love of my life, whom I love more
than anything, to my beloved wolf, the modest genius,
my darling rabbit, for whom I've always written, and
for good reason, the same inscriptions for 13 years!
Kiss:
hervé

In 1991, we'd known each other for thirteen years but only had eleven in which Hervé had a chance to inscribe a book to me.

"Modest genius" comes from back when we were always blowing things out of proportion; he'd proposed defining me by the category of "genius," a noun I couldn't accept that was purportedly balanced out by the adjective "modest."

My Manservant and Me, 1991.

*to my beloved wolf, on this day that's wonderful
because it's the one when I see you again:
hervé
July 28, 1991*

There were times, at the end of his life, when Hervé
would have rather, I think, that I not see him.

He'd been delighted that I'd read *My Manservant and
Me* as a burlesque version of *To the Friend Who Did Not
Save My Life.*

Vice, 1991.

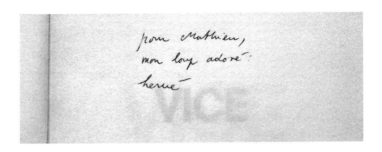

for Mathieu,
my beloved wolf:
hervé

I'd forgotten that this book which was printed in August 1991 was inscribed.

Cytomegalovirus and *The Man in the Red Hat* came out after Hervé's death but they weren't, strictly speaking, posthumous works: he'd finalized the text and, in any case for *Cytomegalovirus*, gone over the galley proofs (I had as well). In this text, he'd oddly lashed out at someone close to him and I asked him if the target of those lines had read that. "Yes," he said. "Well, now you can remove them, can't you?" I said, and so he did.

After having read *The Man in the Red Hat*, I confessed to him that I didn't remember that trip to Russia he'd mentioned and he got a chuckle out of my being so clueless, that trip had never happened. That book really touched me and I made that clear enough to him that, just after his death, his friend Thierry told me: "Hervé was so happy that you liked the book that much." And it was I who was happy, of course.

Thank you, Christine Guibert, for allowing me to reproduce Hervé's inscriptions (and the photo "Berlin-Est").

My sincere thanks are due to Jeremy Ellis, Benoît Loiseau, Daniel Lupo, Clément Ribes, Peter Sokolowski, and Alex Valente for their assistance with various minutiae. And to Hedi El Kholti, an editor I very much consider a friend, for this beautiful meditation on friendship.

ABOUT THE AUTHOR

Mathieu Lindon is the author of nineteen books and a staff writer for *Libération*. *Learning What Love Means* received the prestigious Prix Médicis in France in 2011 and was the first of his works to appear in English.

ABOUT THE TRANSLATOR

Jeffrey Zuckerman is a translator of French, including Jean Genet's *The Criminal Child* and Hervé Guibert's *Written in Invisible Ink: Selected Stories*. In 2020 he was named a Chevalier in the Ordre des Arts et des Lettres by the French government.